C000072375

12 Shades of Breast Cancer
Our Story, Our Way

Dr. LaKeisha McGee

12 Shades of Breast Cancer Copyright © 2020 by

The Scribe Tribe Publishing Group. All Rights Reserved.

All rights reserved. No part of this book may be reproduced in any form or by any electronic or mechanical means including information storage and retrieval systems, without permission in writing from the author. The only exception is by a reviewer, who may quote short excerpts in a review.

Cover designed by Justin M. Carey Designs
Photography by Bella Dawn Photography, Kristyn B. Brown,
Journi P. McGee, Shoot by Scoop, Derrel Todd & Mike Watson Films

Glossary terms courtesy of American Cancer Society (www.cancer.org),
Cancer.Net (www.cancer.net), Breast Cancer.Org (www.breastcancer.org)

Dr. LaKeisha McGee
Visit my website at www.lakeishamcgee.com

Printed in the United States of America

First Printing: October 2020
The Scribe Tribe Publishing Group
P.O. Box 1264 Homewood, IL 60430

THE SCRIBE TRIBE
PUBLISHING GROUP

ISBN-978-1-7352568-3-2

Some have endured alone.
Some have been afraid to share.
Some have felt hopeless.
Some have been embarrassed.
But not my sweet angel, Lady Ashley.
She was so strong, such a fighter.
Full of courage,
Full of encouragement,
Full of hopes and dreams.
She never gave up; she fought until the very end.
Such a beautiful person with a beautiful smile that lit up the room.
So loving and kind. Her spirit will live on forever. We love you Ashley!

Ashley Alexia Smith (Dec 24, 1993-Jan 5, 2019)

This book is dedicated to all the Ashleys who fought to the very end and never gave up!

Acknowledgements

I am who I am because of the creator and I'm eternally grateful. Thank you, Yah, for choosing me. During this most difficult time, I saw his promises like never before. He showed up and showed out, stretching his hand near and far while touching the hearts of many.

To my village, my family, friends, sorors (skee-wee): You all loved me, inspired me, believed in me, took flights for me, called me, cooked for me, went to chemo with me, paid bills for me and even prayed for me when I couldn't do it for myself. Thank you all for having my back. I witnessed Yah's true agape love when complete strangers came to my rescue and I'm forever humbled. Thank you.

To my ancestors, the shoulders I stand on, those that slept before my birth (Hattie B.) and those that literally breathed life into me (Arthur, Walter, Priscilla, Charles): Thank you all; I'll forever pay it forward.

To my mom, my bonus present: I could never repay you for all the sacrifices you've made for me and my children. Thank you for teaching me true, unconditional love. You will forever be my Shero, the wind beneath my wings, the perfect mom for me. I love you.

To my four piece--Jason, Jordan, Journi' and Jouris: Mommy loves you so much. You have taught me how to fly. Thank you for being passengers and enduring every ride I've ever taken. You all are the air I breathe.

How blessed I am to have two fathers! Daddy (James Ricardo): Thank you for giving me life and for always encouraging and believing in me.

PawPaw: Thank you for doing life with me. Because of you, I am an assured woman who believes she can do anything. I wish heaven had a phone just so I could hear one more lecture. I miss you so much! Always, your only daughter. (James Earl McThomas - Aug 1, 1948-Sept 30, 2015)

Contents

Foreword

Make Each and Every Moment Count

Since 2008, My wife and I have been an advocate for teens with our organization, Saving Our Daughters and a little later, we created the Cinderella Program. The Cinderella Program is a fine arts program under SOD, with high-profile mentors such as co-founder, actress and singer, Keke Palmer, who has supported the cause since she was 11 years old.

Saving Our Daughters took on a deeper meaning in 2009, when our youngest daughter, Iliss Marie, was diagnosed with a malignant brain tumor. In 2011, my world splintered when I lost my beloved daughter to cancer at 12 years old. Since 2014, the engine of our work has been fueled by the loss of our daughter. Somehow, amid the heartbreak, I have emerged with a daily prayer of gratitude and an important message for parents.

A parent never fully gets over the loss of a child. Some pain will always be there, but we get through the days by remembering that our dear daughter belonged to God first, and He entrusted us with her care. That's why my message as a proud father is to tell your children that you love them every day. Our sons and daughters are a gift.

During these trying times we are in, I commend the authors—Ms. Lakeisha McGee and the amazing survivors in this incredible book, *12 Shades of Breast Cancer*—for their inspirational journey to be a beacon of hope for women and men of color that have been affected by breast cancer and to inspire them to make a difference as well.

Our Iliss Marie was very spiritual as she often read her Bible and devotion most mornings. She encouraged and prayed for the other children in the hospital. She often woke up at the 3am hour and started speaking of God's love and praying for others. The nurses that witnessed Iliss' faith were often in awe and were encouraged by her strength.

In the overview of this life-changing book, I wanted to pull this quote: *"As of now, society has been told that there's no known cure to cancer, but my prayer is that the powers that be realize that life is more precious than money and release the cure."*

Our Iliss Marie taught her friends to love, be strong and never give up! Most of all, everyone that knew Iliss and her young journey learned about God. That's my prayer for all who read *12 Shades of Breast Cancer.*

Please enjoy the read. Be encouraged and be empowered!

~Curtis Benjamin

www.savingourdaughters.org

We Kicked Cancer's Ass!

Cancer is the result of uncontrolled normal cells growing in the body, dividing at uncontrollable rates, and turning into tumor cells. It is the second leading cause of death globally, estimated at 9.6 million. According to the National Cancer Society, as of 2020, 627,000 will be diagnosed and die from breast cancer. That's one in every eight women in the U.S. In comparison to Caucasian women, African American women have a lower diagnosis rate but a much higher mortality rate for several reasons. The main one is the lack of early detection which is the key to increasing the chances for successful treatment. If breast cancer is found early, there are more treatment options and better chances of survival. Another area of concern is clinical trials, according to the Mayo Clinic. In 2017, they observed a decrease in the recruitment of minorities over the past 14 years. There is much concern over why this is so. Is cancer too profitable? This has been a popular debate as many believe cancer is a big money maker. It's over a trillion-dollar industry and no one wants to let it go. With the advancement of technology, the ability to send men to outer space and the advancement of medicine, I, like so many others, am wondering where's the cure. As of now, society has been told that there's no known cure to cancer, but my prayer is that the powers that be realize that life is more precious than money and release the cure. This anthology gives you a look into the lives of twelve survivors who kicked cancer's ass. No, it wasn't easy, but we were committed to winning. Our hope is that sharing our truths will inspire you to keep fighting.

God's Grace and Mercy

Survivor: Vonda Robinson

Diagnosis Date:
November 1, 2006

Diagnosis:
Infiltrating Ductal Carcinoma
Grade 3/3

Age at Diagnosis: 36

Treatment Plan:
Left Breast Mastectomy
4 Lymph Nodes Removed
Port Insertion
9 Rounds of Chemotherapy (Adriamycin and Cytoxan)
9 Rounds of Radiation
Right and Left Breast Reconstruction
TRAM Flap
Tummy Tuck

I was a 36-year-old single mother of two teenage sons, living on the west side of Chicago. My oldest was a sophomore and his brother was a freshman. At the time, I was working at Loyola Medical Center in Maywood. I had just worked a 12-hour shift and was tired as usual.

Scheduled to work another shift later that evening, I went home to get myself together. As I was showering, I felt a lump in my underarm area. Initially, I freaked out a bit, but then I brushed it off thinking that

I was just tired and imagining things. I continued with my morning and I waited until I got to work to speak with one of the ER doctors that night. Dr. Grano examined me and found a pea-sized lump. There was some pain in the area, but she told me to not be alarmed and instructed me to set up an appointment with Dr. Yao at the Women's Health Center. So, I scheduled the appointment for the end of October when I would be on vacation.

From October 1st to October 20th, the lump grew to the size of a golf ball. Dr. Yao sent me to get an ultrasound. When the ultrasound technician asked me to lie on my right side, the mass bulged out the side of my left breast and resembled a small fist. I literally started freaking out when I saw the lump poking out like that. Within the next few days, Dr. Yao called me and said that she wanted me to come in to do a biopsy. She explained that a biopsy meant that a slit would be made on the side of my left breast where the lump was. Next, they would snip a piece of the mass and send it to the microbiology lab for testing. Dr. Yao told me that it would take four to five days to determine if the mass was cancerous. My test came back in two days; the mass was malignant. On November 1, 2006, I was diagnosed with Infiltrating Ductal Carcinoma Grade 3/3 Breast Cancer.

I remember that day so well. I was standing in the middle of my bedroom floor on a flip phone. That's how long ago that was! I was so shocked at the results the doctor gave me. I thank God that I was not alone when I received the news. My boyfriend at the time dropped everything to go with me to get the biopsy, and he was right there when I got the call from the doctor sharing information that changed my life. God knows exactly when to send someone to be there for you.

Dr. Yao scheduled me to meet a team of doctors consisting of an oncologist, a chemotherapy doctor, a radiation doctor, and resident doctors that would be working with the more seasoned doctors. That date was called Orientation Day. I received a white binder with all the doctors' names, pictures, and profiles. That day, I met my oncologist, Dr. Kash. Dr. Kash was the one who initiated my treatment plan and set the whole process in order. We sat and talked and Dr. Kash asked my opinion on some things. He was saying so many things that I didn't understand, so there were more questions than anything. Patiently, Dr. Kash answered all my questions. One thing that I vividly remember is when he said, "You're going to be just fine! Keep going no matter what happens. Do not stop your treatments." When he said that to me, I felt positive that I was in good hands. I met the rest of the team and they set up all the tests that I would need before I even started chemo. I had to do a MUGA scan, a PET scan, multiple CT scans, and some blood draws. OMG! I felt so overwhelmed with all the tests and blood draws that I had to complete. By God's grace and mercy, I was able to get everything done with no findings of anything wrong. Besides the lump in my breast and my axillary area (arm pit), I was perfectly healthy.

The department where I worked was in the back of the emergency room, so I was exposed to nearly every possible scenario. I saw intoxicated patients, the psych patients, the GSW (gunshot wound) patients, the cracked chest patients in the trauma bay and babies being flown in to receive treatment. I saw it all! Yet, I was anxious to get back to work after being on vacation. I guess I just wanted to hold on to the normalcy of working when everything else around me was changing so swiftly. My first day back, I shared my diagnosis with all the doctors who were close to me. One physician, Dr. Kenny, told me to leave and not to come back to work. She explained that after my first round of chemo, I was going to feel like shit. Dr. Kenny kicked into mama mode as she gave me instructions to apply for my FMLA and not return to work until my treatment plan was complete; she refused to take 'no' for an answer. I couldn't do anything but comply. The hospital is one of the most germ-infested places, and I couldn't afford to be exposed to all of that. So, I followed what she said, and I didn't come back. I filled out the paperwork and got my FMLA process going.

At that time, my family knew nothing, so I set up a time to talk to my mom and sister. During an informal lunch at IHOP, I told them what was going on. My mother knew something was wrong, but she wasn't alarmed. She just had a look on her face that indicated that she wanted to know what the game plan was. My sister, Tammy, had a scared and worried look on her face, but she simply asked the same thing that my mother was thinking. "What's the game plan?" I told them both that I had two boys to live for and my boys were the only things that I was concerned about. They needed me and I needed them. We scheduled a time to bring all the kids together so we could talk to them.

I had three nieces: Ashley, Brittany, and Caprice who were present when we shared the news. They understood everything and cried as we told them. My nephew, Daniel, was too young to understand what was going on. My baby boy, Avery, was scared and just cried. My oldest son did not cry at all. They both turned to their social settings as an outlet to cope with my diagnosis. The oldest one was running the streets trying to find his way, while the baby boy was hanging out with friends. I went to both of their schools and informed the principals of the situation at home. Just in case anything happened while they were at school, they would have a support system there as well. As time went on, I was relieved that they knew what was going on, but I was also genuinely concerned for my boys. Those two were my world and I knew I had to survive for them. My prayer life went even higher. I didn't know what to say or how to say it, but I just prayed that God would keep me here a little while longer for my sons. I spoke positive words over my life, my sons' life, and the medical teams' life.

Dr. Kash set me up for my port placement. A port is a device that is placed in your main artery to help get the blood draws needed for your tests, as well as to administer your chemo. It was recommended that I get a port because my veins rolled, and it was hard to insert needles into them. Having a port readily in place made it a bit easier. (I still have my port in a cup on my dresser.) Placing the port was hard to do because they could not even get a vein to give me any medicine or anything. Eventually, they were able to get a line in and start the process of inserting the port. The port was placed in my upper right side close to my shoulder area. That joker hurt and if I leaned on it, tapped on it, or brushed past it, there was pain. My boyfriend was waiting for me to come out and had been told that a port insertion would only take thirty minutes. Because of the difficulty they experienced with finding a vein, it took two hours. Once my port was inserted, I proceeded to get dressed to go home when I received a call to set up my first chemo round.

I had a total of nine rounds of chemo. I believe I started chemo at the end of October or beginning of November. The nurse informed me that twenty-four hours after my first round my body would change. She told me that my hair would come out and the chemicals would turn my nails dark. She explained that my feet would become numb at the bottom and how it would affect my toenails. As she was talking to me, I thought how strange that as chemo was being pumped into me to kill one bad thing, it was also killing and damaging good cells as well. But as Dr. Kash told me, I kept going no matter what happened. My prayer life went even higher. I was talking to God every day about things that were happening to me and how confused I was.

The day I was scheduled for my first round of chemo, I had to first have my port flushed with Heparin. I could literally taste the Heparin and it messed me up. Afterward, I went next door to start my chemo journey. Later that day, I was at home resting and I rubbed my head. My hair started coming out in clumps in my hand as I cried like a baby. I cried so hard because I couldn't believe my hair was falling out. Once my crying spell was over, I called my boyfriend at work and told him that my hair had come out. He rushed home and looked at me and told me everything would be okay. He shaved the rest of my head and then he hugged me tightly. It was a scary moment.

I talked to my mother and sister throughout my ordeal and they prayed hard for me. They knew me well, so they were aware of what I was going through emotionally and physically. After my first round of chemo, I was supposed to go back to the hospital to get the Neulasta shot. The shot would have boosted my energy, but I didn't go back to get it. I wasn't aware that not getting that shot would have such a negative effect on me. Thinking I could just get it after my next round of chemo was a big mistake. I got so sick like I had the flu with body aches and all. Eventually, I made my way to the emergency room because I had a high fever and that's a no-no with chemo treatment. A fever could have potentially opened me up for infection. After being in the ER for hours, I was admitted for a two-day stay. I had to receive blood because my blood was low, and I was also pumped up with antibiotics to get rid of any infection that was present. While I was in the hospital, I learned that Dr. Kash had left Loyola Hospital. Honestly, that was devastating and that hurt my feelings. I was very angry thinking, "*How dare you leave me and not tell me?*" But God had my angel in transition to meet me that very next day!

I was praying that God would send me someone who was compassionate and thorough with their patients. I really needed someone who would take their time with me and not just pass me by like I felt Dr. Kash did. The nurse that was taking care of me told me about Dr. Gaynor, who happened to be a nun. During their daily rounds, Dr. Gaynor came in with the residents to examine me. I explained what I had experienced which led me to be admitted into the hospital. Dr. Gaynor was the first to step in and introduce herself and when I laid my eyes on her all I saw was white (purity). Her hair was salt and pepper, but more white than black. Her overall appearance was neat, clean, and classy. She looked at me and I just smiled and whispered, "Thank You, Jesus."

In a brief conversation with Dr. Gaynor, she informed me that I had gotten sick because my chemo medication was too strong for me. It was not just solely because I did not return to get the Neulasta shot. She reassured me that I was doing well as she agreed to take me on as a patient. Thankfully, my awesome nurse team had been talking to her about me. Dr. Gaynor eased my anxiety about changing doctors, letting me know that it was a common occurrence. As she spoke to me, she stood at the foot of my hospital bed. When our conversation ended, she grabbed my big toe, shook it, and said, "See you soon." I thought that was a personal touch from God confirming that I would be okay and that I was in good hands. God knows what He is doing, and He certainly knows what His children need.

Every time I was scheduled for chemotherapy, I first had to get blood work done then see my oncology doctor and then do chemo. That was my routine for two and a half months. I was annoyed and tired, but God. I was angry and aggravated, but God. I wouldn't wish chemo on my enemies. I saw old people with oxygen tanks who could barely walk taking chemo. I saw babies from nine months of age to toddlers doing chemo. Now that right there hurt my heart. No child nor senior citizen should have to go through that torture or pain. I did all that I could for them and that was to pray.

As my chemo treatments were coming to an end, I had an appointment with Dr. Gaynor. She had to examine me to make sure that I was okay to move to the next step — a mastectomy. I would have to see Dr. Yao again to schedule my mastectomy surgery to remove my left breast and the tumor under my left arm. I finished chemo in March of 2007 and three weeks later I had my mastectomy. On April 4, 2007, I was admitted into the hospital and my mom and sister were there before I went into surgery. I requested the chaplain, Al, to come. I knew Al from working in the ER; we used to laugh and talk with each other to make the night shift pass quickly. He prayed for me and anointed my head before I went into surgery and then he went out to talk to my family as I was going to surgery. My mom and sister kissed me, and I was off to surgery. My surgery took four hours to complete. In addition to the tumor under my arm, four lymph nodes were removed from my arm pit because they were infected with cancer. A clamp was placed to close off the lymph nodes to keep my arm from swelling. Surprisingly, I was not afraid because I knew God had me. However, I was a little nervous because I had never been in surgery before. But I was a survivor!

I woke up to my mom and sister arguing about waking me up after surgery. That was hilarious, but the pain was greater than my laugh. I had two drains coming out of my left side breast area that were painful as hell. I was wrapped up like a damn mummy and in extreme pain. I couldn't move, but my first words were, "Thank you, Jesus. I made it!" Again, the amazing staff took care of me until I was discharged from the hospital days later. Dr. Yao assured me that everything went well and that she would see me in the clinic in a week. I was taught how to measure and record information, as well as how to clean the surgical areas. At my follow-up appointment, my mummy wrap was cut off. Dr. Yao examined me and told me that I was doing well and that it was time to get my rest. I was given complete instructions on what to do and what not to do after the surgery. Eventually, my energy increased, and I was able to do more walking and moving around the house. I slowly began eating more and it felt great. The negative side effects I experienced were numbness in my fingertips, toenail darkness and loss of my taste buds. I also found myself feeling confused and extremely fatigued.

While I was going through everything, I sent my oldest son away to military school in Urbana, Illinois. That was so heavy on my heart because he needed to leave Chicago to do better for himself. I was worried about him and he was so worried about me, but he communicated with my mom while I was in the hospital. My baby boy was going to school and coming home taking care of me. It was hard for him because he didn't know what to do, but he learned and did an awesome job. During my post-surgery resting period, my oldest son had family day in Urbana, so I rented a car and my son, boyfriend and I took the three-hour drive there and back. I needed to see him, and he was dying to see us. I was still weak and limited to a lot of things, but I went anyway. That day of visiting my son was amazing!

I went to see Dr. Yao again while resting. During that visit, my drains were removed, and I was informed that I would indeed experience some swelling in my left arm from the clamps. Also, during that visit, I was scheduled to see the radiation doctor. Dr. Vijayakumar scheduled me for my nine rounds of radiation and I took radiation every Thursday for nine weeks. My skin became very dark and hard and I was sore under my arm as well as my left breast area. Towards the end of radiation, my skin began to peel and become painful during my radiation treatments.

My breast reconstruction surgery was scheduled for the end of May. I was nervous and anxious, so I asked the chaplain to pray over me and the surgeons again before I went into surgery. As it had been for my first surgery, my mom and sister were there with me for support. However, I didn't have the nicest nurse staff. I asked the nurse to hold my hand and she declined. She told me they were too busy for her to hold my hand, but she went and got my family and I felt at ease again. Once the surgery was completed, I was wrapped up like a mummy again, only that time with four drains—two on each side. It was painful as hell!

Dr. Vandevender was the plastic surgeon who reconstructed my right breast and created a left breast with a nipple. That surgery was massive because I had a TRAM flap. To perform the TRAM flap, the surgeon went back into my left breast area and constructed a breast because I didn't want any implants. Fat from my lower stomach was taken to create my left breast. Essentially, I had a tummy tuck. Reconstruction of my right breast was done to match my new left breast. Yes! I had a new set of perky boobs and a flat stomach which is every woman's dream! (lol) I was doing well enough to be discharged from the hospital on bed rest for a month with doctor appointments throughout the month of June. As the month ended, I prepared myself to go back to work. I went back to work on July 1, 2007. I was happy to see my co-workers and they were excited to see me.

I named this chapter *God's Grace and Mercy* because as you read my story you can't help but see how God held me from start to finish. I had no insurance issues. In fact, I had two insurances: Blue Cross Blue Shield PPO and a medical card. I paid for nothing on this journey! My mother was incredibly supportive. My sister and I bumped heads a few times, but I just took a break so that I wouldn't be stressed about it. We reconciled and she was there until the end. I learned that my boyfriend at the time cheated on me a few times, but not even that could shake me. I was solely focused on my healing. I refused to let anyone, or anything distract me from getting better and beating cancer's ass.

God's hands were all over my family. God put His loving arm around us and protected my sons and me. Today, I am still cancer-free and a 14-year survivor! I thank God every day. To all my surviving brothers and sisters, be available to anyone who needs you. It may be someone you know or a stranger. Just know that God will put people in place for you to share your story. You never know who your story can help; trust God to give you the words to speak. Remind them that by God's grace and mercy, they too will be victorious! Pray for those families that have lost family members to the fight.

The Freedom Journey

Survivor: Freedom "Free" Lemoi
@free_lemoi

Diagnosis Dates:
February 17, 2007 & June 28, 2018

Diagnosis:
HER -2/NEU
BRCA Positive

Age at Diagnosis: 35 and 47

First Treatment Plan:
Right Mastectomy
5 Years of Tamoxifen
Latissimus Dorsi Flap Reconstruction
Implant

Second Treatment Plan:
Left Mastectomy
Right Implants Removed
No Reconstruction (Flat)
4 Rounds of Chemotherapy
(Chemo Cocktail: Lacn Adria, Cytoxan, Taxotere)
25 Rounds of Radiation

One day in November of 2006, as I was on my way to work on the CTA Greenline, I began to get one of my debilitating migraines. A few stops from my job, I got off the train, went in the opposite direction and headed to the ER because I thought I blacked out. I would get migraines so bad that I needed to get shots in my butt. At the ER, they asked me the reason for my visit, and I told them that my head was hurting so badly that I blacked out for a second. I also told them I could feel my head pulsating. They gave me an MRI to rule out an aneurysm and ran other tests on me. They had me on a treadmill for 15 minutes and hooked me up to an EKG. After the testing was complete, I was told everything looked good and that I was a healthy 35-year-old and needed to take it easy as the migraines could have been stress-related. For some reason, that didn't sit well with me; my gut told me to ask for a mammogram, so I did! Yes, I went to the doctor for my migraine and asked for a mammogram. The doctor again told me I was healthy, and my vitals were fine. He said I shouldn't get a mammogram until I was 40 years old and tried to discharge me. I was adamant and said, "Still, I want a mammogram!" I told him I had a maternal aunt who passed from breast cancer and a cousin who was 42 who was recently diagnosed. The doctor then asked me if my maternal grandmother or mother had cancer and when I told him no, despite my aunt and cousin having had it, he told me it had to be my immediate family for him to refer me to get a mammogram! *Really?* But he saw that I wasn't budging! I told him my mom had five siblings who died before the age of 56. When I said that, he finally scheduled me for a mammogram, but it wasn't until a few months later.

The time finally came for my mammogram; I had no idea how many different uncomfortable breast poses were required. After I finished my mammogram, I waited while my images were reviewed, and it was a long wait. The nurse came back and said that they wanted more images, but by ultrasound. When it took so long for someone to come, I began to think that something was up. I had the ultrasound and was told the images showed signs that it might be cancerous, and I would need further testing. Within a couple of weeks, I had a needle core biopsy. It was uncomfortable but not as bad as I thought it would be. During my biopsies, there were some residents in the room and being the silly person that I am, I told them all to step right up and enjoy the show!

Within a week, I received my results. My phone rang and it was the doctor. I had already braced myself for the worst. She told me that I had cancer! There was a pause, an awkward silence, and then a calmness from me. The doctor, on the other hand, was taking it kind of hard; she apologized and said she hated to give that type of news. If I'm not mistaken, I even heard a tremor in her voice. I think I had to tell her, *the doctor*, that everything was going to be okay. I asked her, "What are you going to do about it?" I'm almost always a calm, positive and optimistic being. I was given the option of a lumpectomy with chemotherapy or a mastectomy. I didn't want chemo and opted for a mastectomy. The elders say, "If you don't need it, get rid of it," and I did. A few days after the doctor told me I had cancer, a private call rang on my phone. I usually don't answer them, but this was after normal business hours of unsolicited calls. When I picked up, it was a doctor apologizing to me. It was the same doctor who told me that I was a healthy 35-year-old and didn't need to be tested until I was 40. He apologized. I am a firm believer in being an advocate for my health. Doctors can learn just as much from their patients as the patients learn from them.

I tried to keep it from my parents and children because I didn't want to worry them, but after telling my sister, she told my parents and my ex told my children. I was calm because no matter how much I strayed from God, I kept the faith and I know He kept me. My sister was pregnant at the time of my initial diagnosis and informed her doctor of my diagnosis and her doctor suggested that she get screened, but after she had the baby and was done nursing.

I had a mastectomy. My treatment was Tamoxifen for 5 years. The first year I experienced symptoms of menopause with hot flashes because of the Tamoxifen, but that was about it. In 2009, after my bi-annual visits, the doctors discovered cysts on my ovaries and a mass on the other breast. Although Tamoxifen was for the treatment and prevention of breast cancer, it could cause ovarian cancer. My sister had just recently been diagnosed with breast cancer as well, but she opted for a bilateral mastectomy. I wished I had done that initially. *Why did I choose to hold on to one breast?* I guess I still wanted to feel like a woman. Since there was a family history of cancer, the doctors recommended that I have my ovaries removed. The doctor asked me if I planned on having any more kids. My youngest was 18 and a brat and told me to get a dog if I wanted another baby! So, I was good on having more children. I had my girl and boy, so I got an oophorectomy. *Yay! No more periods!* I thought I would be happy with that, but that caused nothing but more problems. I was really in a menopausal state then! The next day after surgery, I was in a deep sleep due to the medication but woke up to the thought that I wet myself. My clothes were soaked and stuck to my body as if I was in a wet T-shirt contest. Thank God I had locks, or I would've sweated my hair out. That was not a good feeling. Women should not be in a rush to get to menopause. You have bone loss, night sweats, hot flashes and sometimes a dry va-jay-jay! A year later, my sister also had her ovaries removed. Her doctor suggested my sister, my mother, my daughter, and my other sister all do genetic testing. We did and discovered that we all have the BRCA gene.

A biopsy had to be performed on the mass on my other breast. I had a heart with the initials DJ on that breast. I love me some Dwayne Johnson! But those initials also belong to my kids. During that biopsy, I shouted out, "Don't you stab me in the heart!" The doctor chuckled and told me he would never do that.

A week later my phone rang, but I missed my call. I called the number back and it was the doctor's office. They were trying to contact me to give me my results, but only the doctor could share them with me. The nurse told me he was headed out of town on vacation but wanted to talk to me before he left. She said he must like me because he wanted to make sure he got in contact with me before he left. At that point, I was very anxious, and we were playing phone tag. We finally caught each other, and he shared that the mass was benign. I told him that he had scared me! He was so delighted by me that he wanted to give me the good news before he went on vacation.

In 2012, five years had passed, and I was finally done with Tamoxifen! My oncologist gave me the exciting news that I was cancer-free but suggested that I continue Tamoxifen for another five years. My response was simple. "Uh, no! I am done!"

Second Diagnosis

In February of 2018, I noticed a lump in my armpit and thought it may be from my deodorant, so I called my sister and told her about it. She said her husband had a bump under his arm and changed his deodorant and it went away. I also thought it may have been an ingrown hair or hair bump. After all, that was the side I had a mastectomy on and I passed the 10-year mark, so cancer was the furthest thing from my mind. A couple of weeks passed, and it seemed like the bump went away. Two more weeks passed, and I felt a burning sensation under my arm as the lump began to return. I noticed I had a wire bra on, and it was hitting the knot. I thought maybe the bra could be the culprit. To be safe, I went to the walk-in doctor. She couldn't do much, but learning my history, told me to go to the emergency room. At the ER, they gave me an ultrasound and the prognosis was a swollen lymph node. I was instructed to follow up with my primary care physician. I got a referral from my primary doctor for a biopsy and the second time hit me hard! *How could this happen to me again? I made it past the 10-year mark! I had a mastectomy! How can I have cancer AGAIN, on the same side? Well, I am BRCA positive. That's how.*

That time I cried! Going through it the first time was a piece of cake, but the second time I was told I had to do chemo *and* radiation *and* surgery. The first time it was just a mastectomy and pills for five years! I was told I would lose my hair. When I had cancer the first time, people didn't know it, but going through chemo would make me *look* like I had cancer.

After learning about my diagnosis the first time, I changed my eating. I became a pescatarian. I gave up meat, except fish, and I sometimes would relapse on chicken. I said Jesus ate fish, so I wasn't giving up my fish and seafood. I worked out and transformed my body, I got out of a tumultuous relationship, I had a new leaf on life and became FREE LeMoi. I was free from drama, bad relationships, fear, and after my surgery, cancer-free! I flew on a plane for the first time as an adult. I went skydiving and I am afraid of heights. (I won't do it again though. One and done!) I locked my hair up and my locks grew almost to my butt. I always wanted to move to California to pursue my lifelong dream of acting, so I stepped out on faith, left a good paying job, and moved. I became a lover of life and myself. The name Freedom 'Free' is self-explanatory, but the name 'Lemoi' came to me as I was writing in my journal. One day, I was sitting in bed with a pen and pad while looking out the window listening to the birds sing, and a Target commercial came on with the late fitness guru, Jack Lalang. He was doing jumping jacks and saying, "…and loving every moment of it." I looked around the room and said, "I am," and wrote each word on a line and the first letters spelled out LeMoi.

Loving
Every
Moment
Of
It
I was Free and Loving Every Moment of It!

During my second diagnosis, I kept the faith. Since the cancer came back on the same side that I had the mastectomy, they had to take out the implant, remove my skin and muscle, and leave me exposed with muscle. I had the option of having skin taken from my stomach, thigh or back. I wanted it from my stomach and the doctor said that was the best way to go, but in the same breath, told me I needed to gain ten pounds within two weeks. Since I knew that was impossible for me, (it took me ten years to gain twenty and that was from the Tamoxifen) I told him to take the fat off my back. A Latissimus Dorsi Flap was scheduled. The Latissimus Dorsi Flap was a procedure that took an oval-shaped section from my back and shaped into a breast mound and replaced where my breast once was. So, now when I hit my chest, I say I am patting myself on the back! Had I known then what I know now, I would have gone for the fat from my stomach. My chronic back pains are another story.

My chemo port was inserted in September of 2018 and in October, I began four aggressive rounds of chemo and injections to keep my blood levels up. The first two rounds of chemo didn't bother me much, so I kept working. After the second round of chemo though, my blood level dropped, and I had to get injections to increase my white blood cells for five days. Those injections were worse than having a kid and all my surgeries combined. When I say that I cried, I cried at night and on the way to the doctor pleading not to give me those Zarxio injections. My sister was with me and said she never saw me cry like that before. My body was in excruciating pain!

In between chemo rounds, I would get hydration for an hour via IV. The chemo dries you up like crazy. The chemo made my feet dry, ashy, turn black and made them peel. My feet looked like my dad's! (Sorry dad! But he is diabetic, so he had an excuse.) My tongue had also turned black and by that time, all my hair had fallen out. I was in the shower and every hair left on my body was like it went into shock and fell off. Since I knew I was going to lose my hair, I had my friends cut my locks a month before I started chemo, but it started growing back and was gone. After my third round of chemo, my sister and I stopped to get something to eat, but I got a slight stomachache and told her we could eat at home. Besides the injections that one day, I was doing well until that point. We got home and my sister decided to leave me for the first time since I started chemo. When she left, I went to eat my food. A few minutes later, I had the worst stomach pain ever. I went to the bathroom and couldn't do anything. Then I broke out in a hot sweat. Too weak to walk, I crawled on the floor from the bathroom to get my phone in another room and call my sister. I told her I didn't feel well. (She was gone less than 10 minutes.) I grabbed a fan and crawled with it back to the bathroom in case I had to throw up or got the bubble guts. The chemo tore my stomach lining up! So, for about a week, I was on a liquid diet. Soup, water, Gatorade, and juice. I called the doctor and they told me to take Milk of Magnesia and I was all better.

By the fourth round of chemo, I didn't know if I was going to make it. I kept getting fevers, shortness of breath, my blood count was low, and chemo kept getting pushed back. But I finally did it! I was weak though. On December 19th, I had round four of chemo. I was okay at first but days later, not so much! I got a fever and chills, and my friends lived far away. I texted my neighbor and asked if she could buy me Tylenol, juice and Naked drinks since my throat hurt and I couldn't eat anything. The store was less than three blocks away, but I was too weak to go. At my next visit to the doctor, I told them about my fever, chills, and shortness of breath, and they scared me when they said I should've gone to the ER because I was at risk for sepsis!

Originally, my treatment plan included eight rounds of chemo, but after I kept getting sick, and the doctors told me there was no sign of cancer, I chose to stop after the fourth round. I just couldn't do it anymore. That last round almost killed me. I lost ten pounds in less than a week. I was weak and my body was in constant pain from the shots to increase my blood count.

My sister had to go back to work in Chicago, and I was living by myself in California. My surgery was in August. My parents visited me for a week, my mom stayed until September, my sister came in October and left in November, but I was alone in December and getting weaker. My parents lived in Arkansas and couldn't afford to travel back and forth and suggested I come with them from the beginning. I was being Ms. Independent though. I had a job and a place to keep, but by that time, I was no longer working and fell behind on my rent. When we weren't together, they would FaceTime to check on me, but I would put on a hat because I didn't want them to see me bald.

Finally, I couldn't do it alone anymore. So, after the fourth round of chemo and during the week of Christmas, I called my mom and asked her to purchase a ticket for me. I gave most of my stuff away and moved to Arkansas in January of 2019! I felt better as soon as I landed and saw my mom and dad. In Arkansas, I found great doctors less than three miles from my folks. They did a PET CT scan and saw no signs of cancer! I was done with chemo but would start radiation in April. My daughter moved to Arkansas in 2018, so I was able to see her and my granddaughters! I was happy! I moved there in January and by February, my daughter was diagnosed with breast cancer. I went to Arkansas for my parents to take care of me, but I would also be taking care of my daughter. Thankfully, the cancer was detected early and was stage 0! But considering our history, like my sister, she opted for a bilateral. My daughter took it well since she had watched me go through it twice. She had planned for a prophylactic mastectomy because of the BRCA gene and our history. She had the surgery to get them removed but had the expanders taken out in March of 2020.

My radiation treatments lasted from April until May 13th. That's my birthday! What a great birthday gift to be done with treatment!

Being Free

At the time of this writing, six months have passed since my last radiation treatment and my body is still feeling the effects. I had the Latissimus Dorsi Flap surgery and I regret it. I have chronic back pains and want the procedure reversed. The doctors need to share all the long-term effects as well as short term ones with their patients. It's been over a year since this surgery and I have been dealing with back pain since then.

Having my ovaries removed and being in menopause so early, on top of the Tamoxifen for five years caused me to have osteoporosis. The chemo worsened that condition. The doctors wanted to give me yearly injections, but after research, I saw that it did more harm than good. So, I take supplements instead.

God never puts more on me than I can bear, so I know I can and will get through this. I have a great support system and occasionally we all go out for karaoke. It takes our minds off things and we become free. I like to share my good, bad, and ugly journey with people and respond to their questions about chemo, mastectomy, how I feel, etc. I also talk to other survivors who have already gone through what I am going through and that too has helped me. There is nothing much I can do physically, but best believe, once I get my strength back, I am going to be the best version of myself.

God is using me to encourage others to be strong. I've been through the storm and have come back stronger each time. I remain optimistic and keep the faith. A positive attitude goes a long way. The chemo made me weak and caused weight loss, but I tell myself that God broke me down to build me back up stronger than ever. God brought me to it and with faith, I am going to get through it! My favorite scripture is Mark 11:24: **"Therefore I tell you, whatever you ask for in prayer, believe that you have received it, and it will be yours."** This is one of my favorite scriptures because, for a long while, I thought I was God's only child. Whatever I asked for, I received it. When I moved from Chicago to LA, I had no idea where I was going to live. God put me in an Uber with a talkative driver who told me her landlord was renting a unit and she didn't even charge me for the ride. I had no job and got the place! The address just happened to be my birthday and the address when I made my payment was part of my parents. I wanted a house, and I was renting a one-bedroom house. I won a car after being in California for a month and I met celebrities that I wanted to meet, so I know all things are possible if you only believe!

In hindsight, after having breast cancer twice and discovering myself, I would tell women to be an advocate for their health and know their family history. I don't think 40 and 50 years of age should be the first time you have a mammogram. I think if there is any family history, you should be screened. My daughter was just 28 when she was diagnosed and now her daughters will need to be screened when they turn 18. I just pray to God it skips them and keeps skipping.

In the meantime, I am living **Free and Loving Every Minute of It,** proclaiming that cancer took my breast, not my breath!

Hope is the circle of promise.

The Boob Job

Survivor: Cheryl Brown
@beyoutifulmonarch

Diagnosis Date:
November 20, 2010

Diagnosis:
Stage 1 DCIS — Ductal Carcinoma In Situ

Age at Diagnosis: 46

Treatment Plan:
2 Lumpectomies
Right Breast Single Mastectomy
Both Breast Reconstruction
Fat Graph

The first thing I planned to do was get a mammogram as soon as my health benefits kicked in at my new job. I had been laid off for a total of four months and as a result, I had missed my annual mammogram. Normally, I would go at the beginning of each year. Searching for a job became particularly challenging and my main concern was keeping all my physicians because I had developed a relationship with them for over 15 years. Even when I lost my job, my main concern was to ensure that I kept my appointments – especially all women-related appointments. I was embarrassed because I worked so hard to have quality healthcare, only for it to be snatched away. I could have opted to pay for it with COBRA – but honestly, that was a taxing expense that I could not afford on unemployment benefits.

I prayed that I would land a job soon because the money would run out and so would my faith. Interviews and applications had become a thing of the past, and I went to an interview with so much sadness. I cried in the car after the interviews because I was tired of explaining why I was employable or why I would be a great fit or why I would stand out from the others. Nonetheless, I persevered.

Finally, I heard that one "yes" and I was hired! I was beyond excited! As soon as I filled out my onboard papers and passed my probationary period, I knew the next thing would be to call my primary care physician and make an appointment for all my women's care needs. I had the option of one of the best plans available and while this may sound crazy, I was ecstatic to get all my tests done including that dreaded mammogram.

Honestly, I was also a bit afraid to do so because the previous year, in 2009, my mom had been diagnosed with Stage 1 breast cancer and it was the very first time I had witnessed this horrible disease up close and personal. So, for me to call and make an appointment, was a bit frightening and overwhelming, to say the least. Once she was diagnosed, she underwent surgery, the removal of her breast, chemotherapy, and the loss of hair. Thus, as excited as I was to have a mammogram after not being able to, I was especially fearful of the unknown. I finally got the courage to call the mammography department and schedule my appointment. My heart was racing, but I did it.

I was dating someone at the time and when it was time for my mammogram, he surprised me at the doctor's office and was sitting in the waiting room. That was a big shock and honestly, such a lovely gesture of support. Many women don't have support as I did at the time.

I went in for my scheduled mammogram and waited patiently for the results. After waiting for what seemed like forever, I received a call from my doctor asking if I could come in for additional testing because it appeared that I had some type of abnormal reading. I never felt anything in my breast so that call scared me to death. *What? An abnormal reading? What could that possibly mean?*

My primary care physician referred me to another doctor who told me that I needed to have a lumpectomy because I had calcifications (a precancerous condition) and they did not want to take any risks or chances.

I promise I did not hear anything else after that. The physician had a very high-tech presentation with a nice diagram, images, a woman's breast, and the results of my mammogram, but it was all a blur to me. I scheduled my outpatient lumpectomy surgery and it appeared that after the surgery there were more calcifications and my margins were not clear. The surgeon said he would follow up with "other options." The first option was lumpectomy number two. It was another outpatient surgery, so I did not miss a lot of work and I was glad because, as I stated, I had just started a new job.

My doctor called me on the phone and said that after the lumpectomy, my margins had not cleared, and I needed to come into the office to discuss the "other options." He gently told me that I needed to come in for a consultation on the results of DCIS, which is Stage 1 and only confined to the milk ducts. To avoid any risks of it progressing, I was told that I should consider having a mastectomy. When I heard that news, I dropped the phone, crying hysterically and had to leave the office for the day.

To hear the news was a huge shock and felt so unreal. I was in disbelief because I didn't understand what it all meant. Until I could go in and talk about what the next steps would be, my understanding was limited. I was sad. I was afraid. I was perplexed. I worried about my hair, my weight, my relationship, and everything else. *How could this happen to me? I can't go through this; I just started a new job. How long will I be out of work and what would I do? What would be the "new" normal? I am young. I wanted this relationship to work.* Various emotions danced in my head.

Hysterically, I called my mom to share the news with her but waited to tell my daughter because she was in her last year of college and I did not want to alarm her. I really wanted her to finish strong and knew if I laid that type of news on her, it would upset her. Eventually,

I told her, as well as my friends and received nothing but love and unusual support.

The time came for me to meet with the surgeon and discuss the "other options." Even before they suggested a mastectomy, I met with the oncologist and received information about radiation and the plan to receive it every day for six weeks. Just the thought of that schedule exhausted me, but thankfully, I did not have to have chemotherapy or radiation because of my original diagnosis.

The surgeon shared my diagnosis and what having a mastectomy would entail. Again, because I had gone through this with my mom the prior year, I was as prepared as possible. I met with the plastic surgeon too because I opted to have a lateral mastectomy with reconstructive surgery to follow. I did not know how long everything would take, but I chose to be brave and endure what I needed to do to survive. After we thoroughly discussed each detail, a date for my surgery was scheduled.

We arrived at the hospital on the day of surgery and I was full of all sorts of emotions. I knew this would be a life-changing event. My right breast was removed. My breast…something I had with me for 46 years at the time. *Would someone find me sexy with a foob (a fake breast)? Would I have the same feelings in that breast? How would the new breast look?*

After the mastectomy, I stayed in the hospital for a total of five days. I was not immediately prepared for the reconstruction aspect of the surgery. I had spacers placed in my body to stretch the skin once they removed my breast. It was another six to eight months before I received my implant because my skin needed to stretch, and I needed to heal. So, my appointments to have saline injections in the spacer were a long and tedious journey that happened every week. Camouflaging my breast and hiding behind big tops so nobody noticed that I did not have a breast on the right side was such a chore. I could not wear regular bras; most were medical bras. Finally, my breast healed, and the day arrived to have my implant surgery, I also had my left breast lifted and got a slight tummy tuck. Yes, I had a semi-makeover. I was winning!

I also had to have a fat graph since I had no tissue for the breast that was removed. It was a very painful procedure and I felt it all when I woke up. My tummy and my breast were hurting, and I think my feelings were too. I think I was just tired from everything — the cancer, the surgeries, the journey.

I was restricted from driving for six weeks post-surgery and drains and medical bras seemed to be my new sexy. After my six-week checkup appointment, I noticed something abnormal about my breast. It seemed to droop, and it looked very strange. We discovered that the implant was too heavy for my body, which caused it to droop. Unfortunately, this caused me to have another surgery because my mammary fold had not developed properly due to the size of the implant. That procedure was very tiring, and I was very overwhelmed with emotions because I thought I was on my way to complete healing.

Once I passed the six-week post-surgery mark after that procedure, things began to look up. I finally felt like I was on the road to getting my self-esteem back, which I had lost for a moment. Although I did not lose any hair during that time, my self-esteem took a blow because I felt less than a woman without my breast.
A year and a half later, I had my final checkup and I was all clear! Everything had healed properly, and I was free to wear sexy bras with underwires. I had been banned from all of that for nearly a year. I could not wait to buy my first beautiful set.

My support team proved to be stellar. The man that I was dating at the time assured me that my beauty had not diminished at all and I was no less of a woman because I had undergone that ordeal. That relationship did not last, but he fulfilled his assignment to be there with me and encouraged me to remain beautiful and faithful.

My immediate family was supportive because we had just gone through the same situation with my mom the year prior, so we were up for whatever would come our way. The relationship between my mom and I grew stronger too because we both had the same breast removed. She opted to have a mastectomy, but not the breast reconstruction surgery.

I was able to attend my daughter's college graduation and celebrate her. She was away in school most of the time I was going through this, so when she returned home, I was on my way to complete recovery. To keep her abreast of my progression, we talked frequently, and I sent her videos so she could see me doing well.

Thankfully, I had a wonderful support system and the encouragement was genuine. As I watched many women come in and out of the appointments and spoke to some, many did not have a support system as I did. A woman undergoing this type of thing must have someone right there with them. This can be a ridiculously hard thing to go through alone, especially when it is new to someone.

As I look back on my situation, I know that it strengthened me into the woman I am today. It made me appreciate life in such a different way. There are days when I am certain I could be upset about things and how they have gone, then I reflect on what I went through and, immediately, my mindset changes. I have learned to live unapologetically. I realized that life is to be lived and I could have decided to die in the winter or move onward and upward. I chose the latter.

What I've noticed is that people are shocked when I tell them I had breast cancer and even more when they hear that it was "Stage 0." I am often not put in the same category as other women because I did not have to have chemo or radiation or even lose my hair, but trust me, I still endured the pain and went through a lot emotionally.

I had at least six surgeries from beginning to end and that alone was mentally and physically taxing. Having a mastectomy was extremely hard and painful. My circumstance was not the next woman's and honestly, I did not know that it would be like it was. I felt like a piece of me had been taken. When I look in the mirror and see that my breasts are not aligned, it causes some type of emotions and remembrance of what I have gone through. However, I won't start to feel sorry for myself because I learned a lot about myself while going through that. To this day, I am just thankful that I am alive and well.

I always say, "Out of obstacles birth opportunities." That indeed was an obstacle, but it allowed me to change the way I looked at things, love harder and live life to the fullest. I went back to school and received my undergraduate degree in Journalism so that I could empower women through my writing abilities and skills. I could have decided that my story was not important, but my story is important and necessary. We don't often understand why we go through the things we do, but God does and honestly, even in pain there is joy.

I won't pretend that I have all the answers to questions surrounding breast cancer, but I will say that early detection is key. When a woman gets that call that they need additional imaging, they should go because it may not always be a troublesome occurrence. Many women don't take advantage of their health benefits for whatever reasons; however, breast cancer showed me that not only was my health important, but so was I.

My advice to anyone that has received news about having breast cancer is first to breathe! Receiving a diagnosis is honestly hard to hear and handle, but it's not always something that can't be dealt with. I purposely surrounded myself with people who didn't feel sorry for me and if they did, they didn't tell me. Negative energy affects growth! So, I made it a point to be positive daily. It was a real stretch on some days, but it wasn't impossible. As sad and discouraged as I felt on some days when I had to visit my plastic surgeon, I always looked beautiful and put on nice clothes and scents to make me feel beautiful. I made amazing attempts to get dolled up because if other women saw me rising above the ashes and soaring, it inspired them to do the same. *As a man thinks, so is he! (Proverbs 23:7)* What you feed your soul will grow, so it's best to feed it positive things even when you don't feel it! Writing affirmations, speaking well, and celebrating each day makes the days feel less worrisome! I wish I had a secret potion, or I wish I had a magic wand to make it go away. What I do have is a big hug and positivity because without it you sink, and we don't want that. Breast cancer did not define me, nor did it make me have a pity party. What it made me do was to rise and live. I chose life because my ashes certainly turned to beauty. I encourage you to choose life as well!

My Life, My Journey

Survivor: Tanya Ramsey

Diagnosis Date:
August 31, 2011

Diagnosis:
Stage 0 DCIS-Ductal Carcinoma in Situ

Age at Diagnosis: 41

Treatment Plan:
Left Breast Single Mastectomy
Breast Reconstruction
Implants

It was the year that I decided to work part-time for Chicago Public Schools. The school year was coming to an end and I wasn't quite sure how the next series of events were going to turn out. The administrator in charge decided that my position would be phased out and so I was left without a job. I was stressed out trying to decide what to do because my benefits would terminate at the end of August. So, as any mother would, I made every appointment that I could for my daughter: dentist, optometrist, and pediatrician. I had to so that it would be covered under my insurance plan. The most important appointment that I had to make for myself was for my first mammogram. I was 41 years old and just hadn't made an appointment yet. I am not sure if I was just being lazy or if it was all the horror stories that I heard from others about how painful mammograms were. Nonetheless, I made my appointment.

My mammogram appointment was at Rush Hospital. It was not as bad as I expected. The process was over quickly, and I went home. About a week later, I received a call from Rush informing me that they needed to do additional views as well as an ultrasound on my left breast. Worry began to set in until they told me that I had dense breast tissue and that can be normal, but it could also be more. They also stated that because it was my first mammogram, they did not have anything to compare my results to. I tried not to worry. I am usually the positive one, so I told myself that it was nothing to worry about and that everything was fine.

A week passed by and it was mid-August when I got another call from the hospital telling me that I needed to go back for a biopsy. That's when I really started getting scared. I didn't know what to think. So, again I made the appointment and had the biopsy done. Every day that I waited to get the results was excruciatingly painful. Waiting to know whether I had breast cancer was agonizing! *Do I have it? What stage if I do? How will I tell my family? What will I say to my daughter who's 7 years old? Am I going to die? How long do I have to live?* All those questions began racing through my mind until I was finally like, *"Stop it! You're fine!"*

It was August 31st and I was sitting at home watching TV when I got the call. I answered the phone and the doctor told me that my test results revealed that I had DCIS (Ductal Carcinoma In Situ) of the left breast, STAGE 0. She wasn't empathetic at all; she acted like I knew all about this and that I should know what it meant. I remember just staring at the phone, holding it, and not really saying anything, nor hearing anything. I couldn't believe what she had just told me. I didn't *want* to believe it. I didn't even know what DCIS was. I had never even heard of that type of breast cancer. All I could muster up was an "ok" and I hung up the phone after she told me to contact my doctor.

My mind was going crazy again. *CANCER...the c-word! NOOO!* I didn't know what to say or do because I didn't know anything more than what the rude doctor told me. It took me about two days to gather my thoughts and try to accept my diagnosis. I didn't even know what it meant, so how could I explain it to my family or my daughter? I had to get my questions answered, do some research, and figure out exactly what DCIS was for myself. I called my doctor and told him about my experience and began with my first step, asking questions. It was very comforting to have someone to explain exactly what I needed to know and that was patient enough to answer all my crazy, intelligent, and even my dumb questions. After all of that, I made another appointment for my first consultation for the surgery. That was when I found out that they wanted me to have a mastectomy (removal) of my left breast. I felt like the sky had caved in on me. Another blow. *Ok, what exactly does this mean?* I was in denial and decided to get a second opinion, which I felt was the right thing to do.

I made an appointment at Northwestern Hospital. Going into the appointment, I was already a basket case. I was in the room, but not really there. It seemed as if I was just going with the flow. Everyone at Northwestern was nice. Once in the examination room, the nurse came in and took the routine vitals information. Then she asked if I wanted to do the financial information once I finished with the doctor. I responded 'no' because it was too much for me to handle at that moment. I still hadn't told anyone about my diagnosis, so I was doing everything by myself. The doctor walked in, completed his examination, and told me the exact diagnosis based on the pathology reports that he reviewed. The tears began to flow, and I just couldn't stop crying. It hit me that not only did I have DCIS, but I would also have to get a mastectomy as well. I had to come to terms with what that meant and what that process would look like for my life. I left feeling defeated, scared, and confused. My thoughts were all over the place, but one thing was at the forefront of my mind. *I don't have any insurance!*

I sat on my diagnosis for a few more days until I kind of came to grips with it. It was time to explain it to my close friends and family. I told my daughter first and it was the hardest thing for me to do. I just didn't want her to worry about me. She was in 3rd grade and that was an important academic year for her; I did not want anything to distract her. She was amazing though. Her strength was comforting. She didn't know but she was my inspiration and strength. Once she took it so well, it was time to share the devastating news with my family.

It was September 6, 2011, and it was my mother's birthday. I knew that the family would be getting together and although it was going to be hard to tell them about my diagnosis, I decided to tell my family at my mom's birthday gathering. I knew that it was a crazy time to give that kind of news, but I knew that I would be able to tell everyone at the same time. I didn't want to keep telling the story repeatedly. I waited for my brothers, sisters-in-law and a few close friends to get there and then I told them. They were shocked and scared but I assured them that I would be okay. I promised them all that it wasn't life-threatening and that I would keep them informed every step of the way. It was not like they would have given me another choice anyway. Once I shared my diagnosis with my family, I felt much better. Having the support of my friends and family meant that I would not have to go through my process alone.

It was time for me to start considering my treatment plan. By the end of September, my doctor told me that we needed to schedule my surgery as soon as possible. I told him that I had other plans. Not only had I decided not to have the surgery as soon as possible, but I also decided that I would wait until March after my daughter had taken her standardized test.

I planned to try a holistic approach first. I drank organic juices, took supplements, ate raw veggies, took fever baths, drank lots of distilled water and walked during the day. That lasted for a few months.

Even though I knew that my doctor was amazing and that he was telling me what he thought was best, I decided that I was going to make the decisions for my health. I also felt like I needed to do what I thought was best for me and my family. So, I waited and did things the way I felt I needed to. I don't believe that surgery and medicine are the cure for everything and that was one of the reasons that I decided to do the holistic approach first. I would have always wondered what could have happened if I hadn't tried it my way.

While I waited to officially have the surgery in March, I wanted to document my breast cancer journey on YouTube. It was a hard thing to do because I was very transparent and raw. I told the truth about how I felt and what I was going through. One of my major issues was not having any insurance coverage. I explained and cried about how I tried many avenues to get assistance with no luck. I can't adequately explain the feeling when you need help and can't get it even when you're dealing with a serious illness like cancer. The situation was baffling to me. However, my prayers were answered when a good friend of mine saw the video and was able to get me the information for an organization that assisted with health benefits for people with breast or cervical cancer. That was an answer to my prayers and a weight off my shoulders. I recorded two more segments on YouTube before I stopped because my friends and family just couldn't handle it. They didn't understand that the videos were just how I was feeling at the time I recorded; I didn't feel like that *all* the time. My family is important to me and I didn't want to worry them more, so I stopped my YouTube recordings. My medical expenses were paid with the grant though!

In February of 2012, I received a letter from my doctor. He stated that while he understood why I was putting off my surgery until after March, he was still concerned about the amount of time that had passed by. I had already put the surgery off for five months. Since March was near and my cancer was initially noninvasive, he wanted me to go in for another visit to confirm that it still had not spread. I went in for my appointment and nothing had changed but it was also time to set the date for the surgery. I chose April during my daughter's spring break from school. I knew that she would want to be there so I made sure that it was scheduled for a time when she could be present.

Once the date was set, it became real and I realized all that the surgery entailed. No doing this, no doing that. No driving, no cleaning, no ironing, no cooking, no dishes, no making up the bed and so much more. I had to prepare myself for the six weeks of no! I was blessed to have such a great support system. My friends and family were amazing. One of my sister-friends and old college roommate, Vestina Benjamin, came from New York to help me with all the pre-surgery things. She cleaned my house, shopped for my daughter, ironed her clothes, grocery shopped, and made sure that I would be comfortable while being bedridden for six whole weeks.

On the day of my surgery, my family and friends either drove me to the hospital or were in the waiting room as I was prepped for surgery. It felt so good to know that they were there and that when I woke up, they would still be there for me. So, off to surgery I went.

The anesthesiologist put the oxygen mask on my face and told me to count from 10 to 1. *10, 9, 8, 7…* That's all I remember and then I was out! Next, I was in the recovery room asking for lip gloss because my lips were chapped. The nurse laughed and gave me some Vaseline. I was transferred to my room where my friends and family met me. The surgery had gone well. I had decided to do the mastectomy and begin the reconstruction at the same time. There were tubes and drains attached to my body. My medical care team had to ensure that the blood and fluids were draining properly. I couldn't even drain them myself; I didn't want to either. That's where my sister-friend Angela Bowie came in. She assisted with all my post-surgery care.

Angela was serious about her job! She made sure to enforce the no this and no that rules too. She made sure to measure and drain the liquids and made sure that I was doing everything that I was supposed to. At times, Angela even told people no company because I needed to rest. My mother stayed with me and cooked and looked after my daughter. My cousin, Adam Dunbar, came every day and took my daughter to school for six weeks. He was never late either. There were times when my daughter, Montana, wasn't ready and he had to wait for her. I had the best support system ever and it was with the support of my family and friends that I made it through the surgery.

It felt great to have the support, but they didn't know how I felt on the inside. I had just had my breast removed and that was something to come to terms with all by itself. I tried to remain strong for my loved ones so that they wouldn't worry about me, but I also had to deal with things on my own. There were many nights that I cried myself to sleep. Yes, I was glad to be alive, but my life would never be the same. It's not like you can erase the memories of having cancer from your mind. I also had a daily reminder every time I took my clothes off. The scares, missing a breast and having the draining tubes/balls were all overwhelming at times. Yet, I stayed the course and stayed focused on the result.

After the mastectomy surgery was completed, I had to begin the second phase which was the reconstruction process. The reconstruction process was quite different from just having the surgery. I had to go to the plastic surgeon's office weekly. During the mastectomy surgery, I agreed to immediately begin the reconstruction process. So, during the surgery, they inserted tissue expanders inside of my left breast. These expanders would have the skin that was once my breast gradually stretched so that they could do the implants. At that point, there was no left breast and it looked like that of a 10-year-old boy's chest.

I was also able to choose the cup size that I desired. The doctor and I together chose what we thought would look good for my body type. During my weekly visits, the plastic surgeon would insert a saline solution into the tissue expander. That would gradually allow the tissue (skin) to stretch so that when we reached the desired size, the implants could be inserted. I decided to not only do the left breast but to do the right breast as well. That made it so that there was symmetry and a more natural look. I was originally a cup size C but moved up one cup size to a D.

After a few months, I was ready to get the implants. I had already waited six weeks after the mastectomy surgery to get back to the things that I normally did like drive, clean, and make up my bed and it was time to do surgery all over again. The surgery was on October 16, 2012, so it had been over a year since my diagnosis. I had just returned to work in September and I was ready to get everything back to normal. On the day of the surgery, I had mixed feelings. On one hand, I was ready to get it over with, but I was also excited because my left breast would look more normal. Before the reconstructive surgery, I had to do things to make my breasts look even and it really made me self-conscious. I was always a very confident woman, so that was different for me. I didn't want others to notice that my breasts were uneven.

The breast implantation surgery went very well. Although my breasts still didn't look normal, they looked much better than before.

After surgery number two, I still had one more procedure to go—the nipple reconstruction. So, although I had two beautiful, symmetric breasts, I still only had one nipple. But I couldn't have the nipple reconstruction yet. I had to wait for a few months for the next procedure. I felt like I stayed at the hospital on someone's operating table. Before my diagnosis, I had never had any type of surgery. Honestly, if it wasn't for my daughter, I don't think that I would have done it at all. But that's another story.

The nipple reconstruction was scheduled for January 3, 2013. It had been over 2½ years since my diagnosis and I was finally at the last phase. I remember thinking, *yes this is it!* A round band-aid was placed on my left breast to show where I thought the nipple should belong. Then the procedure began. The nipple reconstruction was an out-patient procedure. I went in in the morning and the procedure was about two hours. Afterward, I went home, and they told me what I needed to do to help it heal. It was like a tattoo on my breast that was supposed to look like a nipple and areola. The areola looked fine, but the nipple wasn't raised like a normal nipple; it was still flat. So, although the nipple reconstruction was successful, I still felt like my breast did not look completely normal. However, I was just glad that that process and all the procedures were over.

Once the last procedure was completed, I thought that I could continue to live my life and get back to normal. But I don't think that there is a "normal" after breast cancer. It was like I felt that I had to enjoy life more, spend more time with the people that I absolutely loved and that I knew loved me the same. Although these were things that I had always done, it was even more elevated. I appreciated the small things more and stressed less, at least as best I could.

Throughout this journey, I suffered some financial hardships. Being a single mother, everything was on me. I didn't have anyone to help me out financially. Yes, I was blessed and grateful that my medical bills were taken care of and that was huge. However, I also had a mortgage, car note and bills as well. My diagnosis came at a time when the only income I had was unemployment and of course that only goes so far. It didn't cover most of my bills. I also contacted my insurance company to find out that I didn't have long term disability, even though I know I selected it during open enrollment. So, I was financially stressed. When I called my mortgage company, they refused to give me a modification, so I was left to do what I had to, which was to not pay the mortgage. This situation was extremely stressful, and I eventually went into foreclosure and lost my home. I think that was the lowest point for me. I had no other options and I was already stressed out from dealing with my diagnosis that I couldn't focus on the house. That was a learning experience for me. I can always get another house and eventually I did. Cars and homes can always be replaced but your life can not!

Going through this experience, I have learned and realized many things. One of the things that I realized was that two people can have the same diagnosis, but their treatments can be extremely different. I didn't have chemo or radiation as a treatment plan. My treatment was the mastectomy and, because I decided to, breast reconstruction. I also am not currently on any medication. When I went to see the oncologist, she wanted me to take Tamoxifen, but it had so many side effects that I refused to take it. Taking that pill would only reduce my chances of reoccurrence by 0.5% each year of taking it. This would be something that I would have to take for the rest of my life, and I didn't feel that the side effects were worth my quality of life. When I asked why I should take it, she stated that it was because I was young (41) but an oncologist also recommended my 85-year-old grandmother, who is also a breast cancer survivor, to take it. So, I made the decision that I didn't want to take the medication. I also had genetic testing and was told that I didn't carry the gene. I was satisfied with that and just didn't want my quality of life to be affected by taking the medication. Thus far, I have been happy with my decision.

Another thing that I realized throughout this process was that my family and friends are awesome. I could never have gotten through this without their support. I was a single mother with a young child at the time and they were my support system. My family and friends surrounded me with prayer, love, comfort and as much support as they could. I remember my brother came to my house to celebrate his birthday in April since I couldn't get out. He may not know how much that meant to me, but it meant the world to make sure that I was included. My friends getting together to pray for me, my friends coming from New York to help me, my mother taking care of my daughter, my cousin taking her to school every day, friends making meals for my family, friends and family cleaning my house for me, and countless other kind and loving gestures is what got me through this journey. I love them tremendously!

Up until this time, I haven't really talked about my breast cancer with many people. I pondered on how I could give back or help others and although I came up with countless ideas, I wasn't ready to share my story. There were people that I had known for a long time that didn't know what I was going through. I think that I just didn't want to be treated differently. People start offering up sympathy or trying to be careful around you and I did not want that. I wanted them to treat me the way they always did. So, I just didn't share my journey. I am emotionally ready now to let others know, who are going through this journey, that it's all about you and how you choose to do things.

If I could advise the next survivor, I would say: (1) Take control of your diagnosis. If something doesn't feel right for you, decide to do things your way, on your time. (2) Make sure that you write down all your questions so that when you go to your next doctor's appointment you don't forget what you want to ask. (3) Know that there are others out there that are going through the same thing. Reach out to someone that you feel comfortable talking to and sharing your feelings. (4) Have them explain everything about the process in detail as well as the things that could go wrong. The last thing I want to say is you will get through this!

We're stronger together.

God Got Me

Survivor: Diane Drew Daniels

Diagnosis Date:
May 10, 2012

Diagnosis:
Stage 2/3 Infiltrating Ductal Carcinoma with
T1N1MO
Age at Diagnosis: 47

Treatment Plan:
Lumpectomy
2 Lymph Nodes Removed
4 Rounds of Chemotherapy
(Doxorubicin, Red Devil)
33 Rounds of Radiation

On Sunday, April 1, 2012, I received an out of the ordinary telephone call from my new primary care physician, Dr. Aruna Kandula. She was so adamant that I attend the scheduled appointment to have my annual mammogram done. I was well past 40 and kept putting it off due to other pressing commitments thinking I was fine and could do it the following year. When Dr. Kandula called and made me promise to have it done the next day, I was scared into action. After her call, I remembered earlier that week I was driving down the street and everything began to look new and surreal. I heard the voice of the Holy Spirit say to me, **"No matter what comes, know that God got you."** I simply said, "Thank you, God," and continued with my day. When I got that phone call from my doctor all I could think of was the message from the Holy Spirit. That's when I received the peace to attend the appointment.

My mammogram was scheduled for Monday, April 2, 2012. A week after my appointment, I received a letter that a more intense mammogram was needed because the radiologist saw something. So, I immediately made an appointment to go to Trinity Hospital for the second mammogram. That night, the Spirit of God reminded me, **"No matter what, God got you!"** My follow-up appointment was just a few short days later on April 16th, and by the 19th, I had a letter to consult my doctor because the radiologist had confirmed his findings.

Nervously, I called Dr. Kandula to schedule an appointment with her for the same day at 10:00 am. She said, "Diane, I had a feeling that you had breast cancer. That's why I was persistent that you get your mammogram this year." Within the next few days, Dr. Kandula sent me back to Trinity Hospital to have a biopsy done. That was the scariest moment for me. I feared so many things, but I was ready to fix whatever was wrong with me. I went to church seeking prayer and looking for a word from God that He would heal me. Honestly, all I can remember hearing is, **"God got you! Trust Him."**

On May 1st, the biopsy procedure confirmed that I had breast cancer. Dr. Kandula referred me to an oncologist, Dr. Rosemary Carroll, and we immediately put my plan of action together. My treatment would include a lumpectomy on June 19, 2012, followed by 4 rounds of chemotherapy treatments and 33 radiation treatments. So many questions began to pop into my mind. *I just started dating a nice guy; how can I continue our relationship? I am off work due to a work injury. How is this going to affect me financially? My daughter lives in another state. How am I going to tell her? How will she take it? How will my grandchildren react? Who will help me?* So many questions but the only answer I knew was **God got me!** In my heart, I knew I was in the fight of my life and I was going to win!

The first person I told was my boyfriend at the time. I shared my diagnosis with him and told him I could not nurture our relationship at that time. I was hopeful that we could pick it up later when I was done with my treatments. However, he was not having it. The man responded to my breakup by saying, "I am not going anywhere. I'm in love with you now so what are *we* going to do next?" The next order of business was to call my only child, Kristin. So, he held my hand when I called my baby girl and told her everything that I had been through and what was about to take place in the upcoming months. She immediately said, "Mommy you will beat this because God knows we need you." I realized then that my life meant so much to so many. Everyone I shared the information with claimed my victory immediately which gave me the strength I needed. No one cried or was sad about the diagnosis, which helped my faith grow stronger. I remember being at the bowling alley and I was talking to my brothers by love, Bryan, Bill and Marc and I told them what I was facing. Together, they said, "Man, sis you will beat this, and your brothers are here for you!" All I could do was cry grateful tears because my biological brothers were deceased, but I had those guys willing to wrap their arms around me and assure me that I had their support.

During my battle, I learned and experienced love in action. So often we hear those three words, "I love you," but love is an action. It does, it shows, and it is. People I had forgotten that I adored resurfaced to help me fight. My college roommate, Carla Caddy, drove 12 hours from Tulsa, Oklahoma to love on me. For all the support and love I received, I will always be grateful. During the storm, God gave me some sunny days.

I knew the fight of my life was ahead of me, so I armed myself with as much information on breast cancer as I could. I began to research and answer so many questions like: Where did it come from? Does it run in the family? Because my mother was deceased, I had to call my aunts to find out about our family's medical history. To my surprise, my grandmother had leukemia when she passed but no breast cancer. My mother passed away from cardiomyopathy, but she never had cancer. Next, I called my aunt that treated me like a daughter, my Auntie Milla. I filled her in on all the information from my test results and I learned that we both had the same doctors. I found out that she was battling the horrible disease of cancer as well. However, she was diagnosed with colon cancer.

Auntie Milla told me, "Diane, you will be just fine. **God got you in His hands!**" She also told me to hold my head up. "Every time you go to the doctor's office, look your best, put on makeup and wear a nice dress. You know how to do it! Grab hold of some faith and God will do the rest!"

Auntie Milla confirmed that no one else in our family had breast cancer. After talking to that amazing woman, I researched more and stumbled upon the documentary that Cheryl Crow conducted on breast cancer and bottled water. At that time in my life, I was notorious for leaving a case of water in the trunk of my car, so when I was thirsty, I could drink water instead of sugary beverages. As I continue to read, she informed people about the chemical (Dioxin) used to make plastic water bottles cause breast cancer in women. I believe it was her movement to push bottle makers to adopt BPA free bottles. Based on what I learned, I chose to use all glass containers to eat and drink from. I also began reheating food on the stove instead of in the microwave. When we use plastic containers to reheat food in the microwave those chemicals are leaked into our food because of the change in temperature that melts the plastic.

Additionally, I read that most chickens sold in America come from other countries, therefore they have a ton of preservatives and are injected with hormones for mass production and faster growth. We cook those chickens thinking it's a healthy choice, yet we are consuming harmful cancer-causing chemicals that our bodies cannot identify and fight off. The more I researched, the more my eyes were opened. I learned that black women are born with fibroid tumors and when we eat harmful hormones in our food, they cause the fibroids to grow in our uterus causing damage to our reproductive organs. Many women who suffer from severe fibroid tumors eventually end up with breast cancer or ovarian cancer. So, after retaining this information I made drastic changes in my life, my eating habits, and my thought process. I still eat chicken now, but I buy Amish meat products. It costs more but it's much healthier. I made exercise a priority and began to minimize the drama, anger, and stress around me. I eliminated toxic people that served no good purpose in my life because I was fighting for my life!

On Tuesday, June 19, 2012 at 5:00 am, I had my lumpectomy at Trinity Hospital. In retrospect, I would have insisted on having the lumpectomy instead of the biopsy. The biopsy took pieces off the tumor for testing to see if it was cancerous or not, leaving it open to spread. Why not take the whole tumor out to be tested? Why leave it in me to spread? So, during the surgery, they removed the tumor and two lymph nodes under my right arm, which was the same side I injured at work in December. I began to wonder if the two could be related.

I followed up a week later with my doctor to find out my status and I was diagnosed with stage 2 going into stage 3 breast cancer. When she said that to me, it felt like God took over my body and said, **"I got you."** I was scheduled for four treatments of chemotherapy starting on July 23, 2012. Every three weeks on a Monday morning, at 8:00 am, I would receive Doxorubicin (Red Devil) in my left hand. I chose not to have a port put in because I was only receiving four treatments. Watching the nurse put that stuff in my hand and feeling it go through my body was unnerving. However, my chemo nurse was the best; she gave me nausea medication first so it wouldn't be so bad. The effect of the first treatment was horrible because a couple of days prior I took a laxative and it began to work along with the chemo meds. There was jet black liquid coming out of me like running water and I was doubled over cramping. It felt like the worst sickness I had ever had in my entire life. I thought I was dying! Yet, every time I called out to God, I heard the Holy Spirit say, **"God got you!"**

By day 2, I could not move out of my bed. My head felt like it weighed an extra five pounds and all I could do was sleep. By the third day, I started to move around. I was able to get in the shower, clean myself up good, and finally eat. The sores in my mouth and down my throat made it exceedingly difficult to swallow anything other than pineapple sherbet and banana shakes. On day four, I noticed my hair was thinning. My face was sunken in and my skin looked horrible. By the weekend, I was sort of back to myself. I was able to go to my part-time job as a bartender, which helped a lot to be around my supportive bowling family.

The next weekend, I was watching a movie with my boyfriend. While he was playing in my hair and massaging my head and my hair came out. I was so embarrassed, but he just said, "You are beautiful. I am not leaving you. I love you." That's when I decided to cut it all off. I didn't want cancer to take anything from me; I wanted it to be my choice! So, the next day I planned for my cousin to cut it all off. I could tell she was nervous because we are more like sisters than cousins, but she made it look nice. Embracing my bald head was hard, especially with no eyelashes. It was extremely hard! But what I found out was that people are compassionate and understanding. When I was preparing for a big party and needed to purchase a new wig, I stopped in a beauty supply store. One of the Asian ladies who worked there came over to me and asked how she could assist me. I told her I wanted to try a wig on and as I took my hat off, she affirmed me by saying, "You are beautiful." She went on to ask me how I was doing. The kind woman even offered me half off any wig that I chose. I was so grateful. Everywhere people went out of their way to be kind to me. I saw love in action on days that I felt like giving up. God would send people to my house to bring me flowers, fruit, and hugs to encourage me. During my battle, I continued to enjoy life with my friends and family. My support system was epic. I received so much support that I often wondered how I could be a voice to help women who were scared, fighting their battles alone.

By my second treatment, I knew what to expect, so I ate a steak bagel for breakfast beforehand, which was better. The nausea was at a minimum, but I had to go back the next day to get Neulasta shots to rapidly boost my white cells. According to my blood work, they were depleted. That medication makes every bone in your body ache for about three days on top of the horrid chemo effects. Luckily, by the weekend, I was able to go to my bartending job again.

Near the time of my second treatment, there was also a 5K walk planned in my honor by the Sisterhood for Life Foundation, founded by my childhood friend Michelle. It was a great honor and so many people supported, donated, and walked with me. For the first time since the start of my journey, people saw me without my wig and lashes. More importantly, it raised awareness for many to get checked and know that they were not alone because I was willing to go with them.

As I continued through my third treatment, I watched my God work even more. He opened so many doors for me, but the one I cherish most was my strong prayer life. When I looked in the mirror and realized all my hair and lashes alike were gone, all I could do was cry out *why*? Mixed emotions flooded my mind, but it was at that moment that I chose to find the joy in my fight, find peace and learn whatever lesson God was teaching me. That battle with cancer will keep you on your toes and sharpen your faith like no other. Knowing God will do it and actually experiencing Him during that time was on a whole different level. It was in those moments that God sent people to come by my house with pure love to make me feel better. Every time the devil would try to torment me about the battle, God would beat him with love and defeat him!

My radiation plan included 33 sessions that started on December 1st. Every day, I traveled thirty minutes to receive a five-minute treatment. I was drained after the second week. God blessed me with a great radiation nurse though. She instructed me to buy some Aloe vera gel and Aquaphor lotion to use twice a day. I never had any discoloration, bruising or damage to my skin from the radiation. My scars are minimal, and I accredit it to the aloe gel and lotion.

Just before my radiation began, my boyfriend proposed to me at Thanksgiving dinner, bald head and all! So, I was actively planning a wedding and completing my radiation concurrently. In January of 2013, I completed my last round of radiation. I will never forget the feeling of completing my treatment plan and first hearing that I was officially cancer-free. That moment in time was gratefulness wrapped in happiness and pure joy. Today, I am seven years cancer-free and grateful to my God for His grace and mercy that sees me through all things.

Every day I am grateful to my God for life and its abundance. Through my battles, I praise God. In my quiet time, I thank God, and in everything I trust Him. God will not allow any weapons that form against me to prosper!

If you are faced with the challenges of battling breast cancer, or any cancer for that matter, know that **God got you**! Know in your heart that it's not your battle to fight; it's the Lord and he will fight with you, for you and because of you. Trust him because **He got you**. He loves us so much and will do what his word says. He will do exceedingly, abundantly above all that we can think or ask! What are you asking him for today? I pray that these words inspire your faith and quicken you to know you are not alone. We stand with you in prayer and in life. When two or three are gathered, God is in our midst! I love you!

Early detection saves lives.

Surviving Strong

Survivor: Shanette Caywood
@pink_survivor0

Diagnosis Date:
October 24, 2013

Diagnosis:
Metastatic Stage 4 HER 2+

Age at Diagnosis: 33

Treatment Plan:
Right Breast Radical Mastectomy
Chemotherapy
(Herceptin, Xgeva, Tamoxifen, Lapatinib & Taxotere)
Breast Reconstruction & Implant
20 Rounds of Radiation
Latissimus Dorsi Flap

Maintenance Treatment Plan:
Ongoing Chemotherapy (Herceptin, Xgeva & Tamoxifen)

At the age of 33, I was young, bright, and vibrant without any worries or concerns at all. Sure, I was still trying to figure out a few things about life, but I was pushing through. I was that person before October 23, 2012. I had just returned from a fabulous Jamaican vacation with friends. While on the trip, I mentioned to my friends that I had a lump in my right breast and a small knot under my arm. At that moment it was not a big concern. Besides, I was away from reality and enjoying the beautiful Jamaican weather, beaches, people and let's not forget the drinks. Upon returning home to reality, one of the girls advised me to be sure to make an appointment to have the lump checked out. I made an appointment with my primary physician and was initially told the lump was a cyst and given another appointment at the outpatient clinic to have the cyst drained. That follow-up appointment forever changed my life.

On October 23, 2012, I was told the devastating news I may have cancer and days later it was confirmed to be cancer. As I write this now, I am taken back to that day. Although it's been seven years, it still seems so surreal. At the age of 33, I went to the clinic with the thought that it was just a cyst, but the moment I removed my shirt, the doctor looked at me without a touch and said, "Ms. Caywood, that is not a cyst." She couldn't confirm anything to be exact at the time; however, the concern in her voice as she spoke and the expression on her face said it all. I was sent for a mammogram, ultrasound, and biopsy the same day. I went to the appointment alone as I expected it to be a regular outpatient procedure. When I was immediately sent for testing fear and anxiety set in.

During the ultrasound process, something just didn't seem right. I thought to myself, *"why are there so many people here for an ultrasound procedure?"* When they started the ultrasound, I was okay at first but after I heard a few different sounds coming from the machine as they began to take pictures, I started crying uncontrollably. I just needed a moment. Everything stopped and everyone got quiet as they gave me my moment and tried their best to console me. Once the ultrasound was done, I called my mom to meet me. I was so hysterical over the phone she barely understood anything I was saying. By the time she arrived, I had made it back upstairs to speak with the doctor again. She discussed more in detail of her suspicion and asked general questions about my health. As I sat in the examination room, I heard her words and tried my best to respond but I was not present at all; I was in a complete state of shock and disbelief. As she continued to slowly speak, I couldn't stop crying. I just couldn't comprehend why something like that would happen to me. Had I been such a bad person or done something so horrible and this was my punishment? My boys were 13 and 5 at the time and all my thoughts immediately shifted to them. *Who will take care of them? How do I tell them what's going on? This is so unfair to them.* I had so many feelings and emotions happening and just hearing the word cancer made me instantly think of death.

After what seemed like the longest day ever in the doctor's office, I pulled myself together as best as I could and tried to find a little positivity and hope. Leaving that appointment, I kept telling myself I would be okay. As my mom and I walked towards the elevator, she looked at me and asked, "What are you about to do now?" My reply was, "I have a hair appointment. Regardless of what, I still need to be cute." And that's exactly what I did—made it to my hair appointment. From that moment I had to keep moving because it wasn't the time to be alone with my thoughts. I had to stay busy and not allow myself to think about the news I had just received. My higher conscience and faith had to lead me through the journey from that day forward.

I wasn't ready to talk about it with anyone and I knew my mom would tell the family what we had just been told at the doctor's office. The salon was my escape from having to talk about it. Once I made it to the salon, my phone started ringing off the hook. I glanced up and saw one of my friends casually strolling in the shop; I knew she had also been told. As my phone continued to ring, I rejected every call as I was not ready to talk about the appointment nor deal with everyone's emotions while still processing my own. I knew I couldn't avoid everyone for long even if I wanted to. However, I was not ready to see them or talk as I knew how hurt they would be from hearing the news of cancer. When I finally got around my family, I could tell they were devastated but tried hard not to let me see it. I didn't speak much about it as I wanted to be normal for everyone and tried as hard as I could. At one point I was no longer able to though. My oldest son had just come in from school and he knew something was going on. There were quite a few people at the house, and no one was conversing. Just the sight of my son immediately broke me. Hearing the news myself was horrible enough but having to share it with my 13-year-old was unfathomable. Yet, I found the strength to tell him what was going on.

My son and I were sitting on my grandmother's bed as I began to share the news with him. I didn't go into much detail; I simply told him that I had been to the doctor earlier that day and was told that I may have cancer. I couldn't get much out after the word cancer as he grabbed me and began to sob. I was hurt for both of us and kept thinking about how unfair everything seemed to be. Nonetheless, I tried my best to comfort my son and told him things would be okay as I tried to hold back my tears.

Within the next few days, I had so many appointments that my family and a few of my closest friends were present for. They were there to ask questions and get an understanding. I certainly needed that because there was so much for me to process. That was something I could never imagine going through alone. Everyone knew my personality and how I didn't like to ask for help with much but in this case, without me saying a word they showed up. We were all going through, and I felt bad because I knew how afraid they were for me and I felt the same for them. Yet, this was a situation none of us could control. Instead, we had to get through it together and to this day we still are.

On Oct 26th, I returned to the doctor to receive my results from all the completed tests. I heard the worst news that day. The cancer diagnosis was confirmed, and it was a stage IV diagnosis (invasive breast cancer that has spread beyond the breast to nearby lymph nodes to other organs of the body). The cancer had already spread to my liver and spine and my stated prognosis was three to five years. My diagnosis was defined as HER2 positive (human epidermal growth factor receptor 2). In this case, the cells make too much of a protein known as HER2. These cancers tend to be more aggressive and fast-growing than other types of breast cancer. I immediately thought death and my mind went back to the question, *"why am I being punished?"* I began crying and apologizing out loud hoping that I would wake up from what I thought was all a bad dream. But that didn't happen. It was all my reality. I could see my family and friends quietly shedding tears and letting me have my moment. I now understand that they didn't know what to say or do, which was fine, because at that moment their presence was everything.

After that appointment, the real fight began. Instead of going with the first diagnosis, more appointments were made for second opinions. My mom and cousin researched to find the best hospitals for cancer treatment and made the appointments. I wasn't in the state of mind to do any of that as calling to make appointments and having to repeat the word cancer repeatedly was too much. I appreciated having my mom and cousin take the lead and together we found a hospital and oncologist we all felt comfortable with from the first appointment. The first appointment with her gave me hope. My family and I all felt genuine compassion from her. We discussed how I did not want surgery unless it was necessary, which later became inevitable. A few different treatment options were discussed, and I decided to receive treatment at the University of Chicago Hospital. The reviews of the hospital in cancer treatment, the compassion felt from the doctor and other staff members, and the fact that it was a research hospital which meant there would be many treatments available including clinical trial meds all played a part in my final decision.

Immediately, I started to lose weight as I was afraid to eat almost anything constantly thinking of what could have caused the cancer. *Was it something I ate or perhaps the birth control I had taken throughout the years?* I tried to examine almost everything I may have done that could have caused it. Cancer was not hereditary for me and from the little I knew about cancer I thought only elderly people got it. I realized almost everything I did had to change if I wanted to survive. I began juicing just about everything and would barely eat anything. I completely changed my eating habits along with other much-needed life changes.

Throughout my cancer journey, I have been on more than a few different chemo meds which were mostly used in combination with another. The first form of medication I was given was a pill Lapatinib/Tykerb (a targeted therapy signal transduction inhibitor, which at the time was a clinical trial med), Herceptin/Trastuzumab (an IV targeted therapy treatment for cancers that have large amounts of the protein called human epidural growth factor receptor 2), and Xgeva/Denosunmab (an injection given to prevent bone fractures and other skeleton conditions). The dosage of the oral med was four pills daily in conjunction with the Herceptin which was an IV med given every three weeks as well as the Xgeva injection given every six weeks. The side effects from those meds were mild but tolerable and mainly caused by the oral med. The main effect was constant itching to the point that my excessive scratching would break my skin and leave scars. The tumor began to shrink almost immediately with the Lapatinib/Tykerb, Herceptin and Xgeva combo. Follow-up appointments were scheduled every three weeks with my oncologist and CT scans were every nine weeks. The tumor shrank from 7 cm to 4 cm which was great. However, after four to five months of being on those meds, the tumor in the breast began to grow again and I was on to another chemo med.

That time my treatment was an IV med Taxotere (a cancer med that interferes with the growth and spread of cancer cells in the body). I remained on the Herceptin and Xgeva. Of the few chemo meds I have been on, the Taxotere was the worst. The side effects were horrible; however, I managed to push through. My cycle for that medication was every three weeks. My treatment days were on Mondays and by Wednesday or Thursday of the week, the side effects were in full effect. I would have flu-like symptoms and felt like I'd been struck by a truck; everything ached from the top of my head to the bottom of my feet. The medication caused me to lose my hair. I recall being in the shower running my hand through my hair and all my hair coming out in the palm of my hand. Ironically, I didn't completely freak out as I was told it would happen and expected it. I just hoped it would be later than sooner. In the beginning, I would wear wigs but never felt comfortable in them, so I went from wigs every so often to head wraps. Then one day I realized this is who I am and want I am going through and went out without a wig or scarf. I thought people would look at me and know I was a cancer patient, but it was exactly the opposite. I honestly don't believe I had ever received so many compliments on how beautiful, strong, and confident I looked. I often joke about this saying I should have gone bald a long time ago.

Another side effect of the chemo was that I could barely eat any food during the first week as nothing stayed down. My stomach was upset almost the entire week. I would manage to eat light foods like soups. Sour candies helped with the awful metallic taste the chemo left behind. My fingernails and toenails became very brittle and broke off. They also turned dark and had a smell. My skin was horrible in the beginning. That med broke me down and the hot flashes from the meds would have me drenched at times. I understood that Taxotere affected every good and bad cell in my body with the hopes that only the good cells would regenerate. After being on the med for a few months the tumor decreased in size; however, it once again began growing. It was devastating to hear the words, "Your current chemo med is no longer effective." It was if I was being told that I was running out of life, time, and options. My oncologist was always empathic and hopeful when having to let me know any news that wasn't good. It was always said in a sense to give me hope it wasn't as bad as it seemed and there was more they were able to do. With that, I was off to another med and it was time to discuss surgery. It had almost been a year on a couple of different meds, and we were not seeing the results we hoped for. My oncologist explained if the primary tumor (the breast tumor) was removed she believed I would have better chances with other meds as it seemed the tumor in the breast was the main issue while the tumors in the liver and bones were under control.

The appointment was made with the surgeon, more tests were done, and the surgery was scheduled for November 20, 2013. Things seemed to always happen to me around significant days. At the time of my diagnosis, it was a few days shy of my baby boy's 6th birthday and there I was again at a week or so from my 35th birthday preparing to have a mastectomy. There was no big birthday celebration, just dinner with my nearest and dearest. The surgery was a radical mastectomy, which is a surgical procedure involving the removal of the breast, underlying chest muscle, and lymph nodes of the axilla. It was a four-hour surgery. For me it seemed I had only been out for five to ten minutes; however, I'm sure for my friends and family it was a much longer wait. I recall waking from the surgery very groggy with a slight throat ache. I wasn't in much pain, just soreness but couldn't move much. I had two JP Drains (a closed–suction medical device commonly used as a post-operative drain for collecting bodily fluids from surgical sites) hanging from underneath my now bare breast area. I looked from under the top of my hospital gown and could see the angled scar from the surgery, it was covered with surgical glue and tape. I didn't have much of a reaction as I realized this was all a part of the process of what I was going through. It took me a while to look directly in the mirror at my bare chest. This was not the same as losing my hair as I had come to terms with that. I was a young woman who only had one breast. *How do I move past this and still feel like a woman?* Again, questions came about. *Why me?* I then realized that was another slight obstacle in the process I would get through and overcome.

Through all I had been through within a year, the mental and physical changes of dealing with a stage IV diagnosis, I stayed hopeful and persevered. This wasn't any different. Instead of allowing things to get me down, I pushed through and became confident in everything. I had to realize the physical did not define me, I had to learn to become who I was meant to be. *"I am not my hair. I am not this skin."* Lyrics from my favorite artist, Indie.Arie, began to resonate with me in so many ways. *"I am a soul that lives within."* I had many resources available while going through my process and now I realized I wanted to be a resource for other women going through. That gave me a feeling of empowerment and a sense of control over my situation. While in church a few years back, I heard, "Someone lives because of me." At the time I felt as though that didn't relate to me but after going through what I had been through, I knew my story of surviving wasn't for me. It was to show others what this cancer thing doesn't have to be or look like.

My healing process after the mastectomy wasn't difficult but the most challenging thing was not being able to move around like I normally could. The drains were removed after a week and within five to six weeks I was getting to my new normalcy of life all while reminding myself that cancer would not become me. I wore a breast prosthesis for a couple of years after the mastectomy, and that was a major adjustment. I was not able to have immediate reconstruction due to radiation being needed and concern that the cancer may not be completely gone from the right side. My doctor explained that we didn't want to chance reconstructive surgery with an implant only to have more complications with the cancer or radiation side effects. I asked several times about breast reconstructive surgery and even went to get another opinion at a different hospital. Though they were willing to do the reconstructive surgery, I understood even more why my oncologist was against me having immediate reconstructive and had finally come to an understanding with that.

Once I was healed from the surgery, I began another chemo med, which seemed to have been my miracle drug: TDM1/Kadcyla (a targeted therapy to treat: HER2-positive metastatic breast cancer). I also remained on the Herceptin and Xgeva meds. After having my right breast removed, radiation and being placed on a new med we were beginning to see long term positive results. After having stable scans for over a year, I once again asked about reconstructive surgery and was approved to proceed. That was huge for me as I realized how far I had come along in treatment. I knew it would be another uphill journey as I would need more than one surgery for the reconstructive process. Thankfully, without difficulties, it came out to be a successful procedure. There have been a few other challenges to come my way but none that defeated me. A stage IV diagnosis is considered a terminal diagnosis and I may be on medication long term. I've had to come to terms with a lot while going through and if I can continue to be me through this journey, I am surviving strong.

Unfortunately, once you are considered in remission or advised you are cancer free it's never the end of the word cancer. The lasting side effects are a constant reminder of what you have been through. Not only the mental part but the physical in which my cancer has left me with both. Celebrating the end and expecting to be completely done with the 'C' word then comes the PTSD (post-traumatic stress disorder), anxiety, muscle spasms and lymphedema (refers to swelling and when extra fluid builds up in your tissue when your lymphatic system isn't working well because your lymph nodes were damaged or removed). These are just a few of the side effects without mentioning the intimate part it took from me. My PTSD affects me more than often and at times I feel as though I've become a hypochondriac as with the smallest ailments I think "has my cancer returned." I get headaches from time to time and think, *"Could this be a brain tumor?"* I feel pain and/or muscle spasms in my breast area and wonder if the cancer in my breast returned. Every pain or ailment I feel I fear its cancer. I also experience anxiety and depression at times. When I think back, all I have endured with this cancer thing I get mad and think how unfair this whole this has been. At times I experience depression thinking of how everything in my life was forced to change in the blink of an eye. When the anxiety and fear kicks in, I have learned to reach out to my circle of sisters that has been through it all. This helps me more than I realize at times.

The muscle spasms I experience are due my Latissimus Dorsi Flap surgery as this was the type of breast reconstruction I opted for. An incision is made in your back near the shoulder blade. Then, an oval section of skin, fat, blood vessels, and muscle is slid through a tunnel under the skin under the arm to your chest and formed into a breast shape. My side effects from this procedure are muscle weakness in my right arm and muscle spasms that hit so hard at times in my breast and back area. When these pains come on, I try my best to stretch it out. I've been advised physical therapy would help however, after having so many doctor's appointments to manage the whole cancer thing I do not want to add another doctor to my list unless it's absolutely necessary.

The lymphedema is one of the main side effects that bothers me as this is more physical. My right arm is slightly larger than my left arm caused by the swelling of fluids in the arm. It's probably not noticed by many however, the fact I know, feel, and see it is enough for me. Wearing long sleeve shirts and jackets are different as the sleeve of the right arm is always a tighter feel and look than the left arm. I have a compression sleeve I wear, but it doesn't help me much. I've concluded this is another lasting side effect I must deal with. This damn diagnosis robbed me of so much but at the same time gave me some unimaginable memories.

During my cancer journey, there have been many ups and downs but far more ups with God's grace and mercy getting me through. As harsh as the side effects were, I moved through my routine of life as much as I could. I continued to work because staying home was not an option for me. I didn't want to stop moving because being still made me feel as though I was not in control and the cancer was winning. From the day of diagnosis, I made it a personal challenge that I would still move through life as best as I could. Thus far, overcoming some of my most difficult times hasn't been all bad. I have experienced so much through something I thought would break me mentally and physically. I didn't recognize my strength and beauty until I was forced to see it and become it. This cancer thing helped me to realize this journey is not about me; I've learned how important it is to help others get through and that is what gives me strength. This journey was about becoming bigger than me and taking on challenges I had never imagined.

Cancer is known as the invisible bully and I became a huge giant over this thing. Instead of allowing my diagnosis to define me, I used it to form me. I decided to join a running group with other cancer survivors and completed a couple of 5K runs. I am active in several organizations as an advocate and mentor. I've had the opportunity to appear in a beauty ad for Ulta Beauty in which my tagline was "Cancer Can't Take My Expression." In the ad, I was able to show what a stage IV diagnosis does not have to look like. I've done one-on-one mentoring as well as panel speaking events on how I have survived through my diagnosis and speaking on what could be different when dealing with cancer as an African American woman. I have become incredibly open in sharing what I have been through in hopes of inspiring the next.

The most exciting adventure was my two-week trip to Cape Town, South Africa as an ambassador with the organization, A Fresh Chapter. This trip was an experience of a lifetime as I visited the continent known as the Mother of all Humanity. I knew my visit there would be meaningful and purpose filled. It was sad to know that as beautiful as this country is, cancer is a stigma and some are shamed for their diagnosis. The healthcare in South Africa is nothing like the United States which makes it difficult for those with serious illnesses. However, through all I encountered in seeing people dealing with different ailments, I saw their happiness and individuals not allowing their circumstances and situations to become them. They had peace and happiness within. I had the opportunity to go to hospital and home wellness visits, speaking, praying for health and continued happiness or just being present and listening to their stories. I had the opportunity to speak at an empowerment event within one of the communities. I was immensely proud to be able to share my story of surviving with hope and how I have been able to get through some of the toughest times by deciding to live with much intent and tenacity. This wasn't instant, but it became clearer that everything I had been through was in preparation for those types of moments. I went on that trip with no expectations and received so much in return. I now say if this cancer thing shall ever return at a dire stage it has given me a life I never imagined, many great friends, family, life experiences, boldness, beauty and a legacy to leave behind for those who have crossed my path to always remember. All my worries and fears with this cancer journey are placed in God's hands. It will always be his will and not mine.

My advice to anyone going through a diagnosis is to try not to let your diagnosis define you. My diagnosis showed me I couldn't control everything that has happened such as being diagnosed. But for those things I can control, I became stronger and took control. Try your hardest to live through it. Love now, live now and laugh now! Choose to survive strong!

Real men wear pink.

Against All Odds

Survivor: Antwone Young
@thereala.m7

Diagnosis Date: December 2013/July 2019

Diagnosis:
Stage 3 Male Breast Cancer

Age at Diagnosis: 37 Years Old/43 Years Old

Treatment Plan:
Left Mastectomy
15 Lymph Nodes Removed
6 Rounds of Chemotherapy

Maintenance Plan:
Ongoing Treatment

My name is Antwone Young, and I am a male breast cancer survivor. Breast cancer is said to affect 1% of the male population. I was not aware that men could get breast cancer until I was sitting in front of a doctor receiving my diagnosis. That information hit me like a massive hurricane. I felt as though my entire life was being torn apart and blown away in the wind.

How could something like this happen to me? I asked myself. *I am not a woman so how can I possibly have breast cancer?* I thought maybe the doctor was misreading the information or accidentally providing me the diagnosis of another patient. The doctor assured me that the diagnosis was correct. *How did I end up in this position? What will I do?* I had so many things running through my mind.

It was spring of 2013 in Chicago, the place where I was born and raised. I was preparing myself for a six-week job that required me to be on the road as a driver. While away on the job, I decided to lose some weight. At that time, I was 257 pounds and had been diagnosed with mild sleep apnea. After having a sleep study conducted, it was found that I would stop breathing an average of 11 times per hour. That was a mild case. The doctor informed me that my apnea was due to being overweight and if I planned on getting rid of it, I would need to shave quite a few pounds off. I knew that I would have some full workdays but could use my evenings and any off days to exercise in addition to making better meal choices. I decided to eliminate fried food and breads in the beginning along with eating salads daily and replacing drinks containing lots of sugar with water.

The changes in diet were particularly important to me because my eating habits were extremely bad. Those diet changes along with an exercise regimen proved to be greatly beneficial to me and allowed me to lose 35 pounds during the 6 weeks on the road. My exercise regimen began light with 30-minute walks after lunch and dinner and some lightweight lifting. I gradually increased my walk time and advanced to jogging for 45-60 minutes daily. I returned home from my work assignment proud of myself and excited for my family to see the new me. We went out and celebrated my return from work and my new look. Losing weight was a goal for such a long time, and I had finally applied myself to get it accomplished. That gave me a greater sense of confidence in myself and empowered me to continue to push myself.

About a week after returning home, while jogging on the treadmill, I noticed a small brown stain on my shirt. I thought little of it as it was a tiny stain on my left side near my pectoral area. I started to notice the stain on my shirt every day after leaving the gym. It always appeared on the same side. *How could this happen? What is causing this stain?*

One day after taking a shower, I decided to apply pressure on the left side of my chest to see if I could identify what was causing the stains. To my surprise, applying pressure caused a small amount of fluid to discharge from my chest or nipple area. It was a watery brown fluid. That raised a lot of concern for me because it is not normal for men to experience discharge from the chest. I was curious about the underlying cause of that type of discharge, so I did what every sensible person would do—I asked Google! Everything I found suggested cancer and it sent me into a panic. I held myself together the best way I could until I was able to see a doctor. It was suggested to me that I go to the hospital to get things checked out. That's exactly what I did. Proceeding a conversation with a doctor at the hospital, she ordered a series of tests over the course of the following weeks, including an ultrasound and x-ray.

The results at that time revealed that my chest was creating multiple cysts and she did not know why. She said that it was probably some type of infection and gave me antibiotics. She felt that the antibiotic would help the problem. After a few weeks of taking the antibiotics, there wasn't any improvement in the growth of the cyst or the discharge. I expressed my concern to her, and she said that the antibiotics could take more time, but I should not continue taking them as I had enough in my system. She stated that she would order a mammogram and biopsy to have it checked for malignancy if there were still no improvement over another few weeks. Unfortunately, there was still no improvement and we had to do the mammogram and biopsy.

Once the results were in from my mammogram and biopsy, my wife, Teefa, and I went to learn the findings.

In December of 2013, I was diagnosed with stage 3 breast cancer. I was devastated. Cancer had claimed the lives of several close family members and friends in my life over the past 5-7 years. Everything that I had witnessed others experience while battling this illness suggested to me that my life was ending. I was only 37 years old. *How can this be happening to me?* Pondering over the words that had just been spoken to me seemed to be eating away at my stomach. My head felt heavy and my vision temporarily blurred. I began to question my faith in God. *Is this how my story ends at age 37?* I was not ready to accept that as my reality.

I could see the troubled look on my wife's face and that took my spirit to a dark place. As I sat and soaked in self-pity and pain, I began to think about my wife, children and loved ones that depended on me. *How will my passing affect them?* I did not like the way the sadness made me feel so I decided to say a prayer, pull myself together and prepare to fight. My family and friends, both those living and those who had passed away from this illness, would not want me to give up. *I must use this as a moment to be the example of not giving up. My children need to see me fight so that they know to never give up no matter what happens in life.* That would be the biggest challenge of my life as it would require me to keep myself in a positive mental space.

In that moment, I reflected on the words of John Maxwell when he said, "Winning is an inside job." This means whenever we see a person winning on the outside in life, it is because they possessed the necessary tools or ingredients to first claim victory on the inside. We all have seen various types of sporting events or competitions where a less talented person or someone who is physically inferior to a faster, stronger, taller, or even more experienced competitor, still takes home the victory. Was it luck or did they possess something on the inside? I absolutely believe that a person can be such a winner on the inside that no outer conditions can defeat them including weather, skillset of another individual, location, time etc. None of these can stop a person from achieving victory or success. The world witnessed a five-foot seven, Spud Webb win an NBA Slam Dunk Competition in 1986 against Dominique Wilkins, Gerald Wilkins, and Jerome Kersey, who were all taller and stronger. Spud Webb possessed something on the inside that empowered him to take home the trophy. *I will need to reach deep within myself and find peace with my current situation if I am going to be effective in my fight.*

There I was, in January 2014, sitting with my oncologist and having a conversation about the suggested treatment plan going forward. The doctor recommended that I have a mastectomy on the left side of my chest along with the removal of 15 lymph nodes under my left armpit. Once I had time to heal from the surgery, the doctor also recommended three months of chemotherapy and lastly, radiation. The doctor felt that we should begin the plan right away and I agreed. I decided to do the operation, mastectomy, and chemotherapy. I did not agree on the radiation. My appointment was scheduled right away, and I was looking forward to getting it over with and moving on with my life.

On February 4, 2014, I had a successful surgery and was held over for a few days for monitoring. The next morning, my doctor came into my room to check on me and take my vitals. During the process, she noticed that my hemoglobin had dropped from a 14 to a 6. I had to be rushed into an emergency blood transfusion less than 24 hours after having a major surgery. It was very necessary but extremely high risk at the same time. I was blessed that the transfusion went well, and I was back on my way to recovery. Two days after the transfusion, I was sent home to heal. It took me two months to heal from the surgery and I was ready to start chemo.

Honestly, I did not like the way the chemo meds made me feel. My chemo regimen was a cocktail mixture of the two strongest chemo meds available at that time. Unfortunately, I do not recall the names of the meds. I was scheduled to receive my treatment at Loyola Hospital in Maywood, Illinois. The treatment was scheduled bi-weekly for a period of three months. The side effects of the meds included, but were not limited to mouth sores, loss of hair, fatigue, nausea, vomiting, kidney and/or liver damage. I did not experience all these side effects, but I did have extreme fatigue, hair loss, nausea and change in skin complexion. The physical crisis that treatment placed me in caused me to be stressed and weak at times.

To protect my peace of mind, I started writing and creating music to unapologetically express my feelings while going through that fight. I also started studying how the food we eat contributes to the way we think and feel daily. The information I found inspired me to start making serious changes to my diet and lifestyle. I started making small adjustments to my diet by removing some heavier meals like breads and fried food. I started gradually taking it further to vegetarian, then vegan and lastly raw vegan. Today, I am 70% raw vegan and 30% cooked vegan food. I juice 64 ounces of fresh greens and other vegetables daily and eat lots of salads. I have also learned to make quite a few raw vegan meals. I thank God every day for blessing me to make these changes to my diet as they continue to save my life beyond cancer.

A scientist at University Of Chicago Hospital once told me, according to research, exercise helps to offset the side effects of chemotherapy. Being blessed to have such information shared with me, I decided to implement a daily exercise regimen. Due to my immune system being compromised from treatment and the illness I was fighting, I needed to do things that empowered my body to continue fighting and building strength. I visited Dr. Sebi (RIP) at his California office prior to his unfortunate death. I was prescribed a plethora of herbs and supplements to aid me in my fight as well.

The most interesting thing I experienced during treatment was how differently some of my close friends and family started to interact with me. Some of them seemed to stop communicating with me once I fell ill. This was a very hurtful and disturbing feeling. I had moments where I would ponder what I could have possibly done to make people treat me differently or stop speaking to me. In my mind all I had done was get sick, which was not my fault and could have happened to anyone. I had to realize that the treatment I was receiving had nothing to do with me as it was all about how those people chose to act once they received the news of my crisis.

Today as a survivor, I have committed a lot of my time to being of service to others in need. I mentor high school teens and provide counseling services to youth coping with trauma. I do public speaking and consult people looking to make healthier life choices as it relates to diet. My experience taught me that self-care is health care and it is in our best interest as human beings to learn as much as we can about how our bodies and minds work. My experience has taught me to establish balance in my life. My experience has also taught me that anything we think or experience that causes our minds and bodies to feel negative energy or stress is an illness because it is not our natural state of being. Early detection of any illness begins with being able to understand what a healthy mind and body looks and feels like and understanding when something we do takes our minds and bodies out of that mode.

I refused to accept death as my fate at that time. Even though death is inevitable, I chose to believe in more life. I chose to make the best of whatever time I have here on this planet and to do as much as I can to make it a better experience for those I meet. Giving a compliment, smile or simply greeting someone can have an amazing impact on a person's day.

I was a part of the 1% of men that get diagnosed with breast cancer. I was not a wealthy or well-educated person in terms of medical knowledge, nor did I know any people that I was close to that beat an illness like cancer. I had all the odds against me in terms of survival, but I am still here. Belief and faith allows us to escape what we see in front of us and focus on the image or picture in our minds. I saw myself being healthy again and refused to believe what I saw in front of me at that time and chose to focus on what I saw in my mind.

In July of 2019, I was diagnosed with breast cancer again. I am currently in treatment and my story is still being written. Praise be to God that I stand here today, grateful, happy and I will be healthy against all odds!

My Faith Fight to Victory!

Survivor: Lisa Boyd
@inspiredbyfaithtees

Diagnosis Date: July 28, 2015

Diagnosis: Stage 2 Triple Negative IDC

Age at Diagnosis: 47

Treatment Plan:
Left breast Lumpectomy
3 Lymph Nodes Removed
Port Insertion
12 Rounds of Chemotherapy
(Cytoxan, Taxol)
32 Rounds of Radiation

I thank God for blessing me to be alive, well, and able to share my testimony of little faith. God said to me, **"If I have faith as small as a mustard seed, I can say to this mountain, 'Be uprooted and removed, and it will obey me." (Luke 17:6)** A little bit of faith is better than no faith at all. And without it, none of this would have been possible. (Hebrews 11:1) I'm so grateful that I used the little faith that I had.

My fight began on July 27, 2015. I was relaxing on the sofa in my living room, watching a movie at 10:30 pm when I heard the voice of the Lord say, "Touch your breast." I ignored it the first time because it seemed weird. Less than a minute later, I heard the voice again say, "Touch your breast." That time it was a bit more aggressive! So, I shrugged my shoulders and shook my head as curious thoughts began running through my mind.

I'll touch my breast. What harm could it do? I sat up and grabbed both of my breasts in my hands and immediately I felt the lump on the inside of my left breast. In disbelief, I stood up terrified and walked quickly to my bedroom. As soon as I closed the door, tears rolled down my face uncontrollably as fear tried to destroy me that night. My mind began to reflect on all the times that my doctor gave me referrals to go and have my annual breast examinations done and I didn't go because of fear! I feared the thought of cancer, so I didn't get mammograms. To me, it seemed like everyone who had mammograms was being diagnosed with cancer and then dying. So, as crazy as it may sound, I feared getting a mammogram. I did not realize at the time that the devil was trying to destroy my life with fear. I didn't want to hear that c-word. It seemed like that was a fight that nobody won. I've seen it take the lives of so many great people, especially two that I loved so dearly—my grandmother and my mother.

I'm so glad that God loves us so much that He speaks to us in unexpected ways. If I would have ignored His voice that night, I would not be alive to tell you that God has a perfect plan for our lives, and He wants us to be healthy and to enjoy the plans He has for us. God reminds us in 3 John 1:2 that it is His will that we live, prosper and be in good health even as our souls prosper. This is especially true when we are in a covenant relationship with Him. God wants us healthy. The world has a saying, "What you don't know won't hurt you." That's a lie from hell because if I had taken those annual mammograms in faith, I wouldn't have had to fight cancer. But because I was pleasing the devil by living in fear of them, I almost lost my life.

The night I felt that lump, I was shocked and angry with myself!! I cried and prayed myself to sleep listening to Dr. Cindy Trimm's prayers on YouTube for peace and comfort. The next morning, I called my mother and explained to her what I had felt; she told me to call my doctor. I phoned my doctor and she told me to come in. That was the day I had a mammogram. After it was done, I sat in the waiting area, anxious to hear the results. The nurse came and said the doctor needed to do more tests because there was indeed a lump in my breast. As the doctor examined me again, she informed me that the lump in my breast was the size of an egg (2.8 cm). She asked if she could perform a biopsy and I said yes with no hesitation. Once the biopsy was done the nurse said, "You can go home. We will call you later in the week and let you know the results."

The next day the nurse called me and said the words that would forever change my life. "I'm so sorry your test results came back positive. You have Stage 2 Triple Negative Breast Cancer. We want to schedule you for a consultation and surgery as soon as possible. Can you grab a pen and paper and write down this information?"

My hand felt like rubber and my usual neat handwriting looked like a 2-year-old's scribble scrabble. I was just that nervous! Once I finished writing the nurse's instructions and hung up the telephone, my hands went up in the air and the tears came pouring down just as they did the night that I initially felt the lump. With my hands lifted and tears streaming down my face like Niagara Falls, I said "Lord, please don't let me die! I know I was wrong for not taking those mammograms that the doctor had written referrals for. Lord, I'm so sorry; please forgive me!"

As I stood there openly repenting to the Lord and leaning on my bedroom dresser for strength, I got quiet for a moment trying to gather my thoughts. A few seconds later, I heard the voice of the Lord speak these four scriptures to me:

1.Beloved, I wish above all things that you may prosper and be in good health, even as your soul prospers. 3 John 1:2

2. All sickness is not unto death but it for the glory of God... John 11:4

3. I was wounded for your transgressions. I was bruised for your iniquities and the chastisement of your peace was upon Me. With My stripes, you are healed. Isaiah 53:5

4. No weapon formed against you will prosper. Isaiah 54:17

As God was comforting me with His word, I lowered my body to the floor and before I knew it, I was lying prostrate in tears. Only that time, I was crying tears of joy as I was listening to God's voice as clear as ever! I laid there quietly for a while praising and thanking God for comforting me with His word. Before I stood up, I remember asking the Lord, "How am I going to get through this? I only have a little bit of faith." God responded, "All you need is a little!" I stood up and laughed! Yes, I laughed because I knew my fight was fixed and all I had to do was go through the process. The process was not always easy, but because I used my faith and stayed positive, I made it through just fine.

Cancer certainly doesn't discriminate. When the devil came for me, I was doing fine in my life. I was married, I had my own daycare business and I was working a career that I loved and enjoyed. I have five wonderful children (4 of them adults) and my 2 oldest sons were newly married and having children. I was so excited to become a grandmother. I also had a few bonus children that I loved like my own. So, it was difficult for me to give them that disturbing news about my health, but I had to tell them and prepare myself for the process as well. I took a deep breath and called each one of them on the phone and said, "I need you to come by the house today; I have something very serious to talk with you about."

Later that day, they all arrived at my house and sat down to hear my urgent news. I calmly told them that I had a lump in my breast and the doctor said that it was breast cancer and needed to be removed immediately. To my surprise, my children's responses were incredibly positive. Almost in unison, I heard things like, "You got this mama!" "You're strong and God's going to get you through this." "Like, you always tell us, trust God!" I smiled and looked into each one of their eyes; I didn't see any signs of fear in my children. At that moment, I knew God was again confirming His word that the fight was fixed, but I had to prepare myself for the process. After they all left my house and went about their day, I knew that I had to live and demonstrate for them exactly what faith in God looked like. That's why it's so important for parents to teach their children about God, especially while they are young, and encourage them to have faith in Him and

His Word. **God informed us to, "Train up our children in the way they should go: and when they're older; they will not depart from it." (Proverbs 22:6)** Then, in challenging times when we need our children to stand in faith with us and relay God's word back to us, they can. My children seemed to have no worries during the process, they really helped me stay strong and focused on winning that fight. A few hours later, my husband came home from work and I shared the doctor's report with him. Immediately, he broke down in tears. At that moment, I knew that I was going to have to be extremely strong for both of us.

Days later, I met with the surgeon at her office. After she examined me, she informed me that because of the size of the lump, I would have to have the surgery right away and possibly my left breast removed. For a moment, everything in me stopped moving and froze! I thought my heart fell out of my chest and hit the floor. I took a deep breath, shrugged my shoulders, and managed to say 'okay' with tears in my eyes. I asked her if there was any way possible that she could save my breast. I was in my second marriage and I loved it when my husband laid his head on my breast. *As a matter of fact, why wasn't he able to detect the lump before I did?* The doctor looked into my eyes and spoke very honestly. "It doesn't look like I can because of the size of the cancer." Adamant to save my breast, I boldly proclaimed to her, "Well, I'm going to ask God if I can keep my breast during this process." She smiled and said she understood. On the drive home, I asked him just that.

It was August 28, 2015, at 6:30 am and it was the day of my surgery. I'll never forget that morning. I woke up well-rested; I slept well because I didn't want anything to go wrong. The reality is that I was just ready to get through my process and win the fight. I didn't want the date to be delayed simply because I didn't get enough sleep. As I prepared to head to the hospital, I paused to repent again. I asked God to forgive me for belittling Him. When I first dedicated my life back to Him a few years before the diagnosis, I should have trusted Him and not feared anything. I felt ashamed of myself for belittling God's power! He convicted me, I repented it, and He forgave me.

When I walked into the hospital at 5:30 am, I was pleasantly surprised to find so many of my family members already there. By 6:15 am, the surgical unit had given my family their own waiting room because the love and the support was so amazing. At 6:25 am, I was dressed for surgery, resting flat on my back, and being rolled into the operating room. I'll never forget the strength of fear that tried to overtake me as my eyes focused on the bright lights when those double doors opened. I'm sure the nurse saw the fear I was trying to fight because she instantly grabbed my hand and reassured me that I was going to be okay while she said a quick prayer. The last thing I remember is taking a deep breath and telling her, "I'm okay, but I don't think the anesthesia is going to put me to sleep that quickly." A few hours later, I woke up and the nurse was the first person I saw. She said the surgery went well and the doctor would be in to talk with me soon. When the doctor arrived, she said, "You're a very blessed woman. The surgery went well, and I was able to save your breast." Even though I was still under the influence of the anesthesia, I smiled and whispered, "Thank you, Jesus," as tears of joy rolled down my face. I knew God was listening to my prayers and honoring my request because I acknowledged my wrongdoing of not trusting Him enough to get annual breast examinations.

When I was finally sent home to finish healing, my doctor scheduled a follow-up appointment for the next week. That appointment determined whether I needed chemotherapy and radiation or nothing further. Well, of course, I didn't want to do chemo or radiation. As far as I was concerned, the doctor said that the cancer was out and it didn't spread or affect anything else in my body, so chemo was unnecessary. I took that to God in prayer as well. The next week at my appointment I was told the news that I didn't want to hear. "Unfortunately, Mrs. Brown, I would recommend that you do chemo. Yes, the cancer is gone but if you do chemo it will kill any other cells of cancer, that I might not have seen." She suggested that I go home and discuss the treatments with my husband and children.

On my way home, as I talked to God, He reminded me that it was my life, my journey, and my decision to make in the end. When I asked Him if I had to take chemo and radiation, He answered,

"It's according to your faith, be it unto you!" (Matthew 9:29) I pondered on that answer for the rest of my ride home and decided to go for the chemo. When I arrived home, I told my husband and then called my children and explained that in two weeks I would start chemotherapy for extra security that the cancer was not hidden anywhere else in my body.

Choosing to go forward with the chemo was a big decision to make because I had my daycare and I had families depending on me to provide care for their children. They were all incredibly supportive and just wanted me to take care of me first. I didn't have any medical insurance issues while I was going through my process because I was under my husband's insurance. However, I did experience a major loss in my income because eventually, I had to stop working. The side effects from chemo made me extremely nauseated, fatigued, and weak every day so there was no way I could keep taking care of the children. I was forced to depend on my husband's income until I got better and that didn't work out well for me at all. My first round of chemo was on October 16th. I told a few of my parents that I could still keep the kids because it wasn't that bad at all. After the three hours of treatment, I just felt like I was walking on clouds. My body felt a little different, but overall, I felt well. So, I continued to keep a few of my babies. The next week of chemo, I felt no different. Since my doctor said that it was okay to keep working while taking chemo as long as I felt good, that's exactly what I did until I couldn't do it anymore.

One morning, as I was getting dressed and preparing for my babies to arrive, I began to brush my hair and ugh! I pulled large handfuls of hair out of the brush. My knees got weak instantly. I grabbed the sink and screamed, "Oh Lord, please help me!" I kept trying to brush my hair into a ponytail, but it kept falling out. I called my cousin who does hair and asked her to come over quickly. When she arrived, she cut my hair low and lined me up. By this time, the few children I kept in my daycare had arrived. Children were like medicine to me at that time and I desperately needed them around. The kids didn't notice anything different about my bald head, but that did not change how I was feeling. I was hurting emotionally. Even though my cousin gave me a cute haircut, I still put on a hat because I felt ugly and the devil confirmed my thoughts. A few hours into the day I heard God say, "You are fearfully and wonderfully made," but I didn't see it.

After the third round of chemo, I had to let the children go because the side effects were becoming much more intense and almost unbearable. I refused to sit around and do nothing though. So, I decided to keep one of my toddlers so he could keep me moving as much as possible. He was busy as a bee every day, but I enjoyed his company. By that time, my hair had fallen out completely, my fingertips and toes were totally numb, and my nails turned dark, brittle, and fell off. My taste buds were gone, and fatigue kicked in like an elephant was sitting on my back every day and dragging me. I walked around the house with a blanket because my body was always cold. I hated the smell of chemo going in my body from the intravenous (IV) tubes every Tuesday. I could smell the medication and it always instantly nauseated me. Every Tuesday I felt like I was going to throw up doing those treatments. But God kept me, and I never vomited.

The smell of fried foods made me sick to my stomach. I know that sounds weird, but I could smell the grease in fried foods, and it made me feel lightheaded and nauseated. So, I kept nausea pills to help me feel better. My choice of foods was mashed potatoes, boost nutrition drinks, grapes, and other fruits and vegetables. I also drank a lot of vegetable smoothies. Whatever foods I could keep down, I ate more of. Another irritating side effect I suffered from was constant nose bleeds and irritating sores in my nose. Chemo was thinning the lining in my nose which explains why I was always nauseated from the smell of fried foods. My sense of smell was extremely sensitive.

During my entire fight, I had little to no spousal support. Yes, the devil also attacked my marriage. But to God be the glory, I was able to stay focused on what was more important to me at the time. That was winning and finishing strong so that God would get the glory and I could go back and inspire others through my testimony that faith in God works. As hard as it was for me to forgive my husband for the things that were going on, I had to for me to live. God sweetly reminded me that forgiving him was for my benefit. So, of course, I chose to forgive him and keep fighting like a lady! My children, my family, and my close family friends, near and far, were my biggest supporters. I had an enormous amount of support aside from my spouse. My mother called and checked on me every morning. "Good morning, beautiful!" I can still hear her sweet, sexy morning voice in my head today. We laughed about that a lot. My children kept me positive and full of laughter. Since my hair was all gone and I was confident without covering my head up anymore, my children started calling me funny cartoon character names like Caillou and Little Bill. I loved it because I have a fun personality and I love to laugh. During those difficult months in my life, laughter felt so good to me. I just wanted to be surrounded by positivity. In fact, I never watched the evening news because I felt like I was fighting enough battles and I didn't need anything negative to get into my spirit.

After 11 rounds of chemo, it was finally over. The nurse walked over to me and said, "You're done!" I looked puzzled and asked, "What do you mean?" I knew I was scheduled for 12 rounds of chemo. She explained that my body had responded so well to the chemo that I did not need it anymore. Before I could get out of that chair, my hands went up in praise as tears of joy and relief came pouring down my cheeks. God had delivered me just like He'd promised at the beginning of the fight! The fight was already won; I just had to go through the process.

Two weeks later, I was scheduled for 32 rounds of radiation. Yes, by that time I was extremely exhausted! I was emotionally, mentally, and physically fatigued from all the chemo treatments, but I was determined to finish strong. I desperately wanted to live because I wanted to share my testimony with the world. I wanted the world to know that faith in God works. I wanted my testimony to build someone else's faith in God! I wanted the world to see God's glory through my battle.

After I completed 32 rounds of radiation treatments on April 15, 2016, I promised God that I was not going to be silent! That's why I started my non-profit organization and inspirational t-shirt line. I also initiated monthly visits to the Cancer Treatment Centers. I deliver care packages and share my testimony of faith with patients. I hope that my story inspires them to exercise their faith. I encourage them to focus on living and seeing themselves victorious. According to God's word in **Hebrews 11:1, faith is the substance of things hoped for, the evidence of things not seen.** My mission is to help them believe God and stay in faith. I know God is a rewarder of those who diligently seek Him because I sought Him diligently for my healing!

After completing chemo and radiation, I immediately fell into depression and fought severe panic attacks that I wouldn't wish on my worst enemy! For an entire year, I had to have major counseling to help me recognize how I was hurting myself. Yes, depression is a sickness that we bring upon ourselves by rehearsing negative thoughts in our mind repeatedly. How I got totally healed and delivered from mental depression was by seeking counseling and drawing closer to God for peace. Today, I have a healthy mind. However, there are other side effects that I'm still overcoming to this day and insomnia is the biggest one of all. Some nights my body just won't completely relax so I can fall asleep. To this day, it's normal for my body to stay awake for 24-48 hours on occasions because I'm restless! There's times when I feel numbness and tingling in my fingers and dull pains in my breast from where I had the cancer removed. Some moments I have issues with remembering simple things and my eyes lashes and eyebrows are still thin. But to God be the glory! I am healed, there are no traces of cancer in my body anymore, and I don't take any medication associated with cancer at all. I only take my regular daily vitamins to keep me healthy and recovering well.

During my entire nine-month battle, I managed, by the grace of God, to be steadfast and immovable in my faith. My spirit was strong, but my flesh was weak. Yet, I wouldn't say that out loud. Instead, I would say, "I am strong in the Lord and in the power of His might." I refused to let any negative words come from my mouth. I know the devil was listening and waiting for me to speak defeat or doubt over myself. Our words have creative power! I encourage you to speak life! Be careful with your words. Death and life are in the power of your mouth and you will have what you say! If you say you can't do it, then you can't. But remember, God says that you can do all things through Christ that strengthens you. Ask God for help before you say anything negative! When I was extremely exhausted from the chemo, burned and uncomfortable from the radiation, heartbroken and humiliated because my marriage failed me, sad because I had to close my daycare and devastated that my mother died, all I could say was, "Lord, help me!" There may be times when you feel disappointed and think that nothing is going right, but don't dwell on those thoughts. Just say, "Lord, help me!" It works and God will show up.

I faithfully confessed the four scriptures God gave me at the beginning of the fight every day. I encourage you to speak these four scriptures over your life every day as I did because they work. They are excellent combat weapons for the enemy.

- Beloved, I wish above all things that you may prosper and be in good health, even as your soul prospers. 3 John 1:2
- All sickness is not unto death but it for the glory of God. John 11:4
- I was wounded for your transgressions. I was bruised for your iniquities and the chastisement of your peace was upon Me. With My stripes, you are healed. Isaiah 53:5
- No weapon formed against you will prosper. Isaiah 54:17

A few other things that I would like to share as you go through your fight:

- Be careful what you listen to or watch on TV and social media.
- Stay away from anything depressing or disappointing. Laugh as often as you can.
- Drink plenty of water.
- Don't be so hard on yourself. Give yourself grace as you go through your process. For instance, if you can do laundry one day but not the next, it's okay.
- When the devil comes at you with any negative words (and he will), tell him what God says! Speak the word!

You are not alone! Live inspired by faith. I love you and you are always in my heart and prayers! I am my sister's keeper! Oh, and that little bit of faith—I used it to destroy my mountain (Luke 17:6) and now I'm determined to keep walking by faith! (2 Corinthians 5:7)

Impossible Decisions

Survivor: DeShonjla Andrea Peterson

@logan2kelsi

Diagnosis Date:
November 22, 2016

Diagnosis:
DCIS Stage 1A (Micro Invasive)
Estrogen, Progesterone and HER 2 Positive

Age at Diagnosis: 39

Treatment Plan:
Port Insertion
18 Rounds of Chemotherapy
(Taxotere, Carboplatin, Herceptin, Perjeta {TCHP})
31 Rounds of Radiation
Left Breast Mastectomy
Breast Reconstruction/DIEP Flap

Maintenance Plan:
Tamoxifen

The Discovery

"Damn, you look good girl." That's what I said to myself as I looked at my newly transformed mom body. I was entering into MILFville. Look it up. My once full and supple nursing mom breasts had shriveled up like grapes exposed to too much sun, but that was okay because I was 60 pounds down. As I marveled at the reflection in the mirror, I began to feel those raisins for my monthly breast exam. I had felt them throughout the year and during my nursing stint and they were lumpy as hell. The doctor told me that it was likely from the full milk ducts. He also gave me a tidbit that my chances of having breast cancer would be reduced by nursing.

Well since you see I have a chapter in this book, clearly that statistic didn't apply to my black ass. I digress. As I felt myself up that October evening, I felt two knots in my left breast. I circled and felt around my renewed breasts again at six o'clock and the lumps were still there. I began pressing and squeezing the area to see if the knots could be moved. I stretched the skin. I turned to another side. I even switched hands to make sure the right hand wasn't tripping. They were still there. I rushed to Kevin—he's my superhero in this story who doubles as my husband—to have him feel my breast. He began sensually discovering the new territories upon my chest with more than his hands. I yelled, "Fool, feel these two lumps?" I started to panic because at the first touch my mind immediately thought, *"Aw damn I have breast cancer."* Kevin confirmed what I felt and so began the most terrifying roller coaster ride from hell.

The next morning, I made an appointment with my amazing gynecologist, who said, "Yes, I feel what you feel," (insert warm, uncontrollable tears) "but relax it is probably nothing." He said, "You are only 39, but we will do your mammogram early just to double-check. Stay calm, your body is in the process of trying to get back to its normal state." Normal schmormal!! That baby girl, Kelsi, was 17 months old. How long does that process take?

The Mammogram

The mammography center was like a spa atmosphere. It had dimmed lights, comfy-ish seats, and pleasant people to greet you. If you were a VIP member and getting "your girls" checked, you went to the back of the breast spa where you had a comfy robe, Earl Grey and other fancy teas on deck, as well as juice and snacks. Most importantly, they had on HGTV, which was my great distraction. As Jonathan and Drew romanticized the idea of a fixer upper, I sat with my mom escaping just for a moment until I faintly heard, "DeSho.. Ms. Peterson." My name is DeShonjla, and the pause after the first one or two syllables usually means it's me. I do my usual chuckle at the attempt to pronounce my name as I stir to go back. The nurse asks,

"How do you pronounce your name?" I tell her to sound it out because it tickles me to see what people come up with. Much to my surprise, she got it right. De-Shawn-Je-la is how you pronounce it. Once people attempt it, I usually let them call me Shonni, pronounced Shaw-nee like the Indian tribe.

The one thing they did right was to ensure that there were numerous stress reducers. From the smiles to the expedited service, to the spa-like atmosphere, it was all perfect. I should have known it was all a setup though. I got back to the x-ray room. They asked me to remove my robe, upon which I had a codependency. The room was cold, the machine was quietly humming, and the nurse was smiling and apologizing for her Arctic hands which were touching my body to move me into position. As I stood between the front and back parts of a sci-fi movie machine that had no doors, I shivered violently. I wasn't sure if it was from the temperature in the room or my nerves. As the nurse moved me into position and manipulated my left breast, she also pulled what felt like my chest wall into the picture. As she lowered the top part of the machine onto my tautly pulled skin, flattening out my already small raisin boob, I began to cry. You will see crying is a theme here. My tear ducts are like overburdened dams being pummeled by tons of water that begin to leak.

Why am I crying? Sheesh—I've had my boobs handled before. Hell, I used to flash these size B's out of Tower A in college. Why the shame and sadness now?

I didn't realize it then, but I was overwhelmed by it all. What it could mean for me. Once they finished capturing my good and bad sides, they took me back into the spa where I nestled back into my mom's arms and HGTV. I was called once more. That time it was to see the doctor. She spoke and pointed to what looked like white squiggly lines everywhere and two black abyss-like circles. *Those are the evil invaders—YOU BASTARDS!* That was pretty much what I got out of her explanation. The doctor said it could be nothing, but I should get a biopsy. Yep, you guessed it; I cried one more time for the people that missed the first three times.

I don't understand. I'm not even forty. When I felt them while nursing was that it? I thought only older people got breast cancer. I didn't smoke. Yeah, I ate/eat bacon and drink from plastic bottles and wear antiperspirant deodorant but shit, so do many other people in this world. How did I get to be the lucky one?

I won't spew facts about how many people under forty are affected by breast cancer because I don't know, but I do know too damn many for them not to be researching why. Truthfully, I didn't give a flying fuck because I didn't want it to be me!

The Biopsy

I walked into the room, they pulled twice, I cried (typical), and I waited. That's all I have to say about that.

The Diagnosis

On November 22, 2016, my husband, my mother, and my father drove me to Mercy Medical Center for the follow-up. I came armed. I had Jesus, hope, my support system, and my prayer warriors on deck for that moment. I entered the doctor's office greeted by this slightly above average height white man with a reassuring smile and crazy soft hands. I sat in the chair across from him ready for whatever was to come. He began to speak and cut right to the chase about the results.

"DCIS, blah blah blah, best cancer diagnosis you could have, HER somebody, advances in medicine... blah blah blah... mastectomy... could spread to the other breast.... if you have a double then significantly reduces... blah, blah, blah.... why are you crying?"

I re-engaged in the conversation realizing that he was talking to me. He was speaking to the me that was crying in front of him and not about the me that was being betrayed by her body. I refocused and locked eyes with him and said "I don't want to die. It's all so overwhelming. You are talking about stuff and it's like you're speaking another language." He then asked about my specific concerns. He explained one by one what it all meant and how they would combat it and how I would overcome it. When I began the process, I was DCIS stage 1A (micro-invasive), estrogen, progesterone, and HER 2 positive. My very loose definition of micro-invasive is when a small amount of the invaders aka bad titty meat (cancer) has moved slightly out of the milk duct. It appeared to be minimal, but if I considered a double mastectomy over a lumpectomy or single mastectomy, he didn't think I would have to do chemo or radiation. That was music to my ears! I needed a new rack anyway with this transformed body. I would be a M-I-L-F by 2017. Did you look up the term MILF yet?

Honestly, it was not that sweet. Initially, the diagnosis and treatment plan were palatable. Before meeting with Dr. Friedman, the doctor I ultimately chose to work with, I did have two other opinions to ensure I was making the best decision for myself.

PAUSE You are responsible for your health. You are your best advocate and you have the right to take the time you need to make the best decision for you. If anyone makes you feel otherwise without hard facts as to the urgency, then you need to consider working with someone who cares not just to cure your cancer, but also for YOU! Your mindset is everything through this process. *UNPAUSE*

The first and third diagnosis had the same treatment plan, but the bedside manner at Mercy was the right fit for me. Did I mention that Mercy is one hour away from me? Despite the drive, Mercy was where I felt most supported and comfortable.

During that time, I wondered what my family thought. My mom and dad cried with me, we prayed, and they let me know that everything was going to be okay. There is something about a parent's love that soothes the spirit and makes you feel as protected as you did as a child. I didn't tell my siblings just yet, but I waited until I saw them face to face on Thanksgiving. I knew it would be hard to tell them.

The night of the diagnosis, Kevin and I put Kelsi, our rainbow baby, to bed and we climbed into bed and wept together. Kevin didn't say much, but the way he held me I could feel just how much his pain matched mine. It's weird how something so life-altering can merge two people together. We were one in a way that I don't know that I have ever felt. Each flowing tear was caught with a kiss of reassurance. Each shiver from pure fear of the unknown was comforted by a tightened embrace. The silence in the dark was deafening; however, with every heartbeat and with each breath shared, I could hear his silent prayers for me championing me, willing me, and loving me to health.

The following morning it was game time. Kevin put on the whole armor of God and began his homework. I was still stuck on WTF mode, but the sun still chose to rise as if life didn't just smack the dog crap out of me. The rest of the week was a blur, but I knew that I didn't want to go into the New Year with this monkey on my back or in my titty I should say; therefore, I got to planning.

I made a swift decision to have the double mastectomy on Tuesday, December 20, 2016. The way I figured it, I would be going into 2017 with a new body, new boobies, and on the mend. The one thing I continuously tried to do was stay positive. Some days and some seconds were harder than others. I had a child that I went through so much to have and a family I wasn't ready to say good-bye to. I am not sure why your mind automatically goes to death, but mine did. My mind also had an, "I don't wanna die" drive-by at least once a day. I spoke to God so much. I knew that my answers would come from my source, or at least a feeling of peace. As the days swiftly passed by, I began to settle into the idea that I was one of the lucky ones, if you can say that. The doctor said he thought that I would only have to have the surgery and do maintenance drugs for five years. It could have been so much worse.

The Sunday before surgery, I could not sleep for the life of me. I went to bed around 10 pm. Monday was going to be my last day in the office and my mind was thinking of all the things that I needed to settle at work before day's end. Eventually, I drifted to sleep, only to wake up two hours later. I went to sleep again, and it was 42 minutes later. By 4 am, I said screw it and got up and went to work. As I drove to work, there didn't seem to be any cars on the road, but I remember vividly that God and I were in a serious conversation. I was speaking aloud, but you know God is the strong silent type. God let me know He was there by placing moments of solace in my spirit. From the time I drove out of my home garage until I got to my office garage, I did not stop talking.

When I arrived at my office building, I was completely at peace with my decision. God had placed in my spirit that I would be okay. It was 5:30 a.m. and I had been at work for about thirty minutes when I had to go to the bathroom. As I walked to the bathroom, I forgot that I had a pregnancy test in my bag that Kevin wanted me to take because he had a dream. When he told me about his dream I thought, *"fake ass Martin Luther King, keep your dreams to yourself!"* I ran back to my office to get it and strolled back to the bathroom.

Wait. Let's go back a day. On Sunday morning, Kevin said to me, "Babe, I had a dream you were pregnant." I told him, "Well, that, my love, is a dream deferred. Didn't you hear the doctor say I have CANCER? Duhhh! God is not going to bring a baby into this mess!" He kept pressing the issue. I was agitated and walked away ignoring him. By Monday morning, I had a pregnancy test sitting on our bathroom sink. I thought, *"I ain't got time for this crap!"* I threw it in the bag and went to work. I knew he was wrong, because after the stress from the first child and how hard it was for us to get pregnant and stay pregnant, it just wasn't going to be the time it happened. We, well the "I" part of the "we" accepted that we would have one child. As long as God allowed me to be here for her, I was A-Okay.

I was feeling very light as I sauntered to the bathroom. Not a soul was in the office or the hallway. I went and did my business while internally fussing about taking the test. As I pulled up my panties, I saw two lines. I mean I couldn't even wipe fast enough before the results showed up. *WTF God? Oh, sorry, God! Thank you, I think. I mean, you gotta be shitting me.* I was pacing in the stall pants mid-thigh trying to figure out how that happened. *Why now? Why in the work stall? Why did he only get me one test?* I needed a damn do-over. I experienced rage, happiness, sadness, confusion, glee, stopped by Anxious Lane right before I landed square in panic mode. I eventually pulled my pants up and washed my hands, but I checked out. I called Kevin, apparently the Ms. Cleo of the family, and he did not pick up. *WTF Kevin?! Ugh!* I kept calling and no answer. I called my parents and they answered. I immediately burst into tears. They had no clue what was going on and as I spoke, my parents just kept saying, "I don't understand you." I felt like a foreign exchange student speaking

English for the first time. As I slowed down and told them what just happened, they said, "Oh, ok." I thought to myself, "*Ummmm what? Oh, ok is not an appropriate reaction! I need to be medevacked to the hospital for a blood test. It's only five something in the morning and how will I know if this freak-out is warranted if I don't have a blood test. God, for real though?! We just had a whole 35-minute conversation. You could have said, "This shit is about to pop all the way off." I mean you gave me no heads up.*

Sheesh! Now, what the fuck am I supposed to do?"

I eventually got in contact with that man, Kevin. His name said with slathering disdain. The one who decided to score a home run. I think he took advantage of my diagnosis and got me knocked up. The nerve of him! Kevin asked, "Well, now what do we need to do?" *How in the fuck am I supposed to know what now? I am new to this cancer pregnancy diagnosis. THIS IS ALL YOUR FAULT!* *insert side-eye* We had to wait until dawn when most humans got up and reported to work. I called my OB/GYN first and said, "I have an emergency, allegedly I just popped up pregnant." This was supposed to be an excitingly happy time and all I wanted to do was throw up and not from morning sickness. The OB confirmed my pregnancy with a "congratulations!" *insert middle finger* *What am I supposed to do now?* I slumped down like a sack of potatoes thrown in a corner. *Is this what being a teenage mother feels like?* After I confirmed the unthinkable, I called the breast surgeon. I left a message detailing the emergency and the need to delay my surgery.

As I left the message, I thought to myself, *how are you not here dammit. It is an emergency! We need to commune with all the higher powers and have my people call your people and talk right now!* That's what I thought, but I simply left a message and hung up.

The Land of Uncertainty

At that point, everything was on pause. I spoke to the doctor and he said, "You have two options." You can either terminate your pregnancy and begin treatment or delay your treatments until the second trimester. *Huh? Did he just say terminate your pregnancy or delay treatment like he was giving me choices of Kool-Aid flavors?* I was flabbergasted. *Is that even an option at 39, in a loving marriage, and desiring a second child? This can't be what I must choose from. How do I choose against my unborn child? How do I not choose Kelsi and Kevin? How do I not choose me first? Mama, what should I do? Kevin what should I do? Dad, what do I do? GOD HELP ME!*

Kevin and I didn't see eye to eye on how to handle treatment, but he supported me and loved me unconditionally anyway. He gave me the "ultimately, it is your decision," but he was very clear that he wanted me if there was a choice between me and the baby. He made it crystal clear that it was not about not wanting our unborn child, it was about wanting me more. He wanted me.

I was stuck. Something in my spirit was so adamant about not terminating. I was so torn though. God had given me this baby so he must have wanted me to have it. Once I told them I needed more time, the doctors simply said, "When you decide, let us know. For now, we will delay the surgery and Happy Holidays!" Do you think they have dealt with this a time or two?

I cried for hours. I began talking to the baby in my tummy reassuring it that I would keep it safe. I felt so alone. *If I don't choose life for my baby, then who will? Who will be the voice on the baby's behalf?* I spent so much time in that space of uncertainty. I don't think I ever came out of it until I completed treatment. That space was by far the most difficult space and time that I have ever been in. Believe me, I have been in some pretty jacked up spaces, but I always had a glimpse of clarity. That time was different. All I had was God and faith, but God wasn't participating in our conversations like I needed. Most times I felt like I was left in the middle of a forest with beautiful tall trees and no matter where I looked nothing was familiar and no direction seemed to be noticeably the right way. I would see sunlight and it would provide warmth from time to time, but it never provided clarity as to where I was going. It was always a deafening silence, even when others were around. No one could answer that for me. It was my decision and mine alone.

Since I was in limbo, I began Googling and searching for people and places that helped people make those decisions. *Who is pregnant with cancer out in social media land?* I could not easily find it. One day someone recommended an organization that supported women who are pregnant with cancer. I had hope. I spoke to them and they linked me up with someone pregnant with cancer, but they were a different ethnicity, they were staged differently, and I could not connect. This saddened me. I guess I thought God would send me a version of me with a clear answer, but no such luck. They then set me up with a doctor who scared the bejesus out of me. She explained that cancer is more aggressive in women of color and that I couldn't afford to not have treatment during pregnancy. She spewed out all these facts regarding how if I have surgery and do not start chemo right away, then the treatment is less effective, or my percentage of recurrence would be increased.

After hearing all the facts and stats of the people who did do treatment while pregnant, I asked what the results for my demographic were who didn't. I also asked did they study any women who chose not to do treatment during pregnancy and their outcomes? The answer was no. Like a piece of paper being tossed by the wind, my hope was getting farther and farther away from me. I remember blogging about it. *What do I do now? Is there nothing that can be done for me during this period?* I felt like the lowest member of the caste system. The OB couldn't do anything until the 2nd trimester, and neither could the breast surgeon. *Is this disease just going to ravage my body?* Along with the increased hopelessness, I added panic and incessant crying. I was fortunate enough to get linked with a holistic doctor who was right by my side through the entire process. Well, she was kind of by my side; she wasn't covered by insurance, so she was by my side when I could afford her. She helped me with supplements and helped reshape my diet. There were a lot of things she took out of my diet. I wondered why the other doctors didn't tell me about these things. There must be a balance between holistic medicine and modern medicine. Why can't it be covered in some capacity? It is not like the woman wasn't a practicing MD. Anyway, for many dollars, she helped me be the best version of me while I awaited treatment.

Along the way, she helped me make the tough decision to undergo surgery to remove the affected breast while pregnant. I asked every single anesthesiologist I knew, which rounded out to three, whether I should have this surgery while pregnant. Each of them told me the risks to my fetus if I have surgery, but they liked my chances. As a result of the never-ending space of ambivalence, when my second trimester came around, I opted to have a unilateral mastectomy to ensure that the cancer didn't continue to grow and possibly spread. The surgery was scheduled for April. The morning of the surgery I remember saying to anyone who would listen, please take care of me and my baby. I prayed and prayed, but I was scared. I was afraid of waking up without Zoë. By now we knew she was a girl and Zoë would be her name. I was wheeled into the room and shaking like a stripper; I was so cold. I remember hearing *Do Me Baby* by BBD in the background and laughing hysterically while the anesthesiologist gave me my dose of relaxing drugs. Once the doctor came in and recapped what was about to go down, those familiar warm tears reappeared. I spoke to Zoë and I spoke to God as I drifted off to sleep. As the doctor held my hands, the last thing I remember was the gentle tears flowing into my ear.

I woke up in recovery one breast down. That, however, was not my primary concern. The first question I asked was if my baby was okay? As I groggily awaited to hear her heartbeat, I told her good job for sticking with me. Once I heard the heartbeat I was lured back to sleep. When I woke the second time, I was in my hospital room, which is where I stayed for the next three days. In plain view, there was a beautiful white rose. It sat on the table on the left side where my old friend used to be. It greeted me in memory of the loss of my good friend. It might not have been as ceremonious as I'm making it, but it was like a homage and I appreciated that.

The next morning the doctor came in and asked me how I was doing. Honestly, I was fine. I felt as if I made a decision and God kept me and Zoë, so all was well. He began to share what he found. He said as expected, you had two masses and we believe we got it all out. However, comma, when we tested your lymph node to determine if it has spread, we found that it had.

Fortunately, only one lymph node out of 13 was positive. As a result, you will have to do chemo and radiation. Cue hot tears. *I can't catch a damn break. Guess I won't be skating through this process.* I thought that by being pregnant that God would give me a break. I then ask as exasperatedly as you can imagine, "Can I please have my drugs to go to sleep? I will deal with this tomorrow."

Happy Birthday!

Leading up to Zoë's birthday I was at peace. I cried just because it was Wednesday. I felt guilty for not being as happy and positive as I was when I was pregnant with Kelsi. I guilted myself into thinking I was crap for not reading aloud more while pregnant, but God said shut up and know that you are blessed. So, I did. As we prepped the house and our bags for Zoë's arrival, I felt excited to meet her.

Zoë was originally slated to be born via C-section on August 21st, but I decided to have her a month early so that I could breastfeed. I remembered the connection that I had with Kelsi through breastfeeding and I wanted that so badly with Zoë. I felt like she was getting cheated already for not staying in the full 40 weeks, and then not being able to nurse for the next 20 years. Well, I nursed for 18 months, but it felt like 20 years. I found myself apologizing a lot to Zoë.

I didn't want her to feel as if I slighted her. I loved her to life. I would trade my life for hers any day of the week and I needed her to feel that love. I cried as I told my dad that I wouldn't have enough time to nurse and that I was cheating Zoë. He said, "Child, if you think this baby is worried about those things you are crazier than I thought. She will know your love whether you breastfeed one day or no days. She will know your love."

On July 31, 2017, at 11:33 am, Zoë Jade Peterson was born. She was perfect. She was ours. God kept his promise and got her here safely. I hired a photographer to come and take pictures of Zoë. One image the photographer captured was of me nursing with one breast. That was such a powerful image. It allowed me to see that even with a lack of a breast I could still nourish my baby. That's really what this journey was most about to me. It was about my ability to protect and nourish our child while relying on God to grant me the desires of my heart and to keep my focus and faith in God. God graciously afforded me that opportunity. It was time to fight!

Let's Get Ready to Rumble!

I got Zoë here safely and now I can fight with all my might to ensure that I stay here. Only four weeks after I had Zoë, I began my treatment. My treatment plan consisted of 6 rounds of Taxotere (docetaxel), Carboplatin, Herceptin, and Perjeta (Protuzumab)(TCHP). Once I finished the six rounds of TCHP, I would continue to do 12 more sessions of Herceptin because I was HER2+. Tamoxifen would then be thrown into the mix. Somewhere post TCHP, I would also be required to do 31 rounds of radiation because that slippery sucker crept into one of my lymph nodes. I was unsure what would happen during this process, but I embraced the treatment plan and said whatever you have for me I am going to make it through. I had two little girls and a sexy man waiting for me. The oncological nurse explained what would happen next and explained all three zillion, one hundred and thirty-six side effects that might take place from the drugs. She then asked me if I wanted to see the floor where I would receive treatment. I was like hell no! I would be there enough to get a bird's eye view of everything.

Ooh, ooh, ooh let me tell you about the first chemo session. I had my bag full of goodies ready to entertain myself for the next six hours. I had hubby on deck. I was ready to color some thangs! The nurse came in and set up my premed drip and started down the laundry list of all they would do. As she spoke, I was incredibly relaxed. It was almost as if I was buzzed from too much holiday cheer. Eventually, I found myself nodding like I was sitting in church at an early service after I had been clubbing all night. I didn't hear a damn thing she said. I asked her why I was so tired, and she said Benadryl. "We will give you Benadryl each time to help you better cope with the side effects," she said. The absolute best part about chemo was that Benadryl induced sleep! I would do chemo all over again if Benadryl was on the menu. Well, that might be pressing it, but I would reminisce about it.

While I had one amazing perk from chemo everything else was hellacious. Four to five days after chemo all the side effects were present and accounted for. I was blocked up. Everything was disgusting to taste. I had diarrhea. My core body temperature also seemed to go up. Even though everything I ingested was disgusting, I drank so much water during treatment because I felt like the side effects went away faster. The side effects visited me every three weeks. By the third round, I began losing my hair. Every single hair on my body. Yep, EVERY hair.

Other side effects that I didn't expect were that my skin would be flawless, I would have hot flashes, night sweats, and an increase in my waistline. Let's talk about that waistline. Aren't chemo patients supposed to lose weight? I thought that chemo made people skinny. It was so superficial, but, man, I was looking forward to a jumpstart back to MILFville. That baby sure did mess that up. However, chemo does cause some to lose weight, but not for these buns. The steroids I was receiving were the culprit. All in all, I didn't have too many horrible side effects. I had no vomiting, nausea, or rashes. I am thankful that regardless of the side effects I was able to go through this process with grace.

I finished the TCHP regimen in December 2017 and they stopped me from taking Herceptin so that I could get ready for radiation. I had to be three weeks out from chemo before they started treatment. I started radiation in early January 2018. It was scheduled for Monday through Friday for 15-20 minutes. The longest part of radiation was waiting and getting set up. From there it was just three breath holds. The first one took a little longer so that we could get the logistics out of the way and I could learn how to lay under the machine. The first day I shed a tear. Not because it hurt or was uncomfortable, but because I felt overwhelmed. I felt like the process was never-ending. It seemed like it was always one more step. When I finished TCHP, I rang the crap out of the bell. I wore bell underwear and socks and everything. I wanted to ring all day! But even though I rang the bell, I knew there was still more to come. I wouldn't be done for about a year. One day, one step, one minute, one second at a time is what I constantly reminded myself. Through it all, I remained in a grateful space.

The radiation tech said, "Mrs. Peterson, when I tell you to hold, you will hold your breath until you hear from me again. Are you ready?

HOLD...BREATHE...HOLD...BREATHE...HOLD...BREATHE.

You are all done. The tech came in and raised the machine and lowered the bed and I got dressed and headed home. I felt nothing. No aches, no burns, no itching. I felt normal. The doctor said that the side effects would be delayed about 2-3 weeks.

I had some darkening of the skin, but then I began to burn. It wasn't a burn as in catch on fire, but more of a bad sunburn. My skin began to peel and was so sore to the touch. That was probably the worst part of treatment for me. I used Silvadene and Aquaphor religiously. It soothed a bit, but it hurt for anything to touch it, even a shirt.

Get Your Hand out my Pocket

Thank you, God, for health insurance. I could not imagine what my costs would truly have been if we didn't have good health insurance. Thank you, God, for my job that continued to help fund us while I was on leave. Thank you for a dual income home. I started with thanks here because there are so many people who do not have any of the above and the costs associated with this crap could destroy you, or not afford you the best treatment possible because someone else would have to eat the costs. That to me is foul! Everyone should receive the same level of medical support when they are battling something that can take their life.

These greedy bastards out here (health insurance companies, drug companies, etc.) make enough money to help supplement some of these costs. I am not a policymaker, nor do I have the ambition to be, but going through this process made me want to lobby for some changes. My husband and I make good money. We have that good federal government insurance that allows us not to have to overpay, but shit got real during this process. Just imagine $40-45 copays for each doctor's visit. All you do during cancer is go to the doctor. In the beginning, you go what seems like every day. So that adds up. Oh, and don't forget to be 39 and pregnant and have an OBGYN that requires you to go see a special specialist, the maternal-fetal medicine doctor, for being pregnant over 35. That could cost you upwards of $135 a month and that's on the conservative side. If I did treatments during pregnancy it might have been more.

Don't get me started on holistic doctors and the insurance companies not covering them and having to pay upwards of $600 a visit. HOLY LAY-A-WAY BATMAN! I was desperate to receive some sort of non-toxic solution while I waited for the first trimester to end so I went the holistic route and I honestly felt better than I have ever felt while going to her, but I paid for that. It got to the point that I burned through my flexible spending account in only a few months. Because of the uncovered, exorbitant costs of the holistic doctor, I did not see her as often as I would have liked.

We always had what we needed, which I am grateful for and we adjusted where we could, but everyone doesn't always have that luxury. Where we really got hit hard was during radiation. Why did I foolishly think that radiation was much like pregnancy? For my OBGYN visits, I only paid a copay when I went to see the "you are old special specialist." On February 1st, I got my first radiation bill. That sucker was $1,500. *Who is going to pay that? Cause like Martin Lawrence said in his show Martin, "I ain't got no ends."* I read the breakdown and looked online for my explanation of benefits (EOB). It broke down everything. Like Jesus, I wept, although for different reasons. That was just one of many bills to come. Go on this expensive journey with me for a minute. Radiation is every day except weekends, and I had 31 sessions. I had to drive to radiation every day which meant gas. I had to go for five days ($200/week) and every 5th day I had to get imaging done ($600/week) and meet with the doctor ($40/week). I had a copay for radiation treatment. Then I had to pay separately for imaging because it wasn't through one of the providers my insurance covered fully, then I had another co-pay for the hospital. Doesn't the doctor work in the hospital?

For about 2 years we were killed by medical bills. Cancer is never a budget line item. The last thing you want to have to deal with in addition to trying to stay alive is the fear that you may die drowning under debt. This is another reason that I believe that people don't care for themselves as they should. They simply can't afford it. This is heart-wrenching. Moreover, I was unclear about how to pay for all of this. I didn't realize that the imaging was contracted out, even though it was in the hospital and I had to pay separately, therefore, they sent my bill to collections. I never received a call that I was delinquent. I had so many bills that came in I wasn't sure that I paid it and I sure as hell didn't have it to double pay.

Most of the people I called to speak to about the bill were nasty. There eventually was one lady who was understanding and told me how to navigate it. She told me I could do a payment plan and it wouldn't send me to collections. I recommend that medical professionals and the hospitals give patients an estimated cost based on their insurance while they are telling them of all the other BS they are going to endure. I know it is our responsibility, but we don't know what to expect or what to ask. Hell, half the time we don't hear what the doctors are saying anyway. It's like Charlie Brown's teacher. "Womp, womp, womp, womp."

After going through my process, I am now on a quest to be financially independent because you can make different decisions when you aren't bound by a lack of financial resources. I pray to be able to set up a non-profit that has many facets to support women going through this process, especially the ones who get the "who in the hell is going to pay this" bill in the mail. That will be just one facet.

Welcome to the Sahara

The most alarming physical issue that happened aside from having one titty, stretch marks, gaining weight and being burnt like ignored toast was that my love box dried out like the Sahara Desert. Man, oh man, imagine wanting to get your swerve on after being placed into a mandated celibacy state. We couldn't have sex while pregnant because of the cerclage that was in place. A cerclage is the suturing in and around the cervix to better support the fetus staying in. Not only were we in a drought we had to use condoms. *We've been raw dawg for… carry the one…many years. What do we do with these rubber things?* That was just another marring of my femininity and womanly awesomeness. I wanted to have sex, bad. Other methods of pleasuring just aren't the same. You may have the same result, but I wanted to have good sex. When we tried, it just wasn't pleasurable for us. It was awkward and it just hurt. I was 40 at the time and they say the forties is your prime. Well, I went from 40 to 80 in a matter of months. I had hot flashes, night sweats, and a dried well. Through perseverance, we tried all the tricks and non-estrogen options I could find, and just like David, we slew that Goliath. We had all types of lubes and creams and got creative with it. Replens worked the best. I also used YES products. Kevin was amazingly patient during this process and never showed his frustration even though he must have felt it. I am sure his hands got super soft from all that lotion. We did what worked for us and now we are back in the saddle, so to speak.

How I Got Over

Throughout this whole process, I trusted myself and God. I knew I was the only one in the end who had to sit with all of this. I didn't always know how things were going to turn out, but I got selfish and focused on me. God gave me the okay through my father saying, "You are no good dead. You need to focus on you and let everyone else deal with everything else." As hard as that was for me, I did. Once I got into the groove of that it was no turning back. Let's be clear though. I was afforded this selfish space because I had my squad and I knew my kids would be safe and protected. My husband ensured that for me. From the very beginning, I felt like I was alone through this process, even though I was loved and had so many around me. The one constant was God's peace stayed with me. I can't say I heard this reverent voice descend upon my ears or even a whisper, but there was a calm that I possessed. I never knew I was doing the right thing. I knew what I wanted. I challenged God to protect me/us or redirect us if we were headed down the wrong path. Look, only God could take that baby away from me. I wasn't doing it and I wasn't allowing anyone else to either. Kevin and I struggled with getting pregnant and keeping babies. We had a late-term miscarriage and gave birth to our 20-week-old baby girl Logan in our bathroom. That was one of the most crippling days of my life. Because of our pregnancy struggles I could not, I would not choose to take her.

Just like God took Logan he would have to take Zoë. I made decisions with the consequences I could live with. I considered the thoughts of others, but I did what God told me to do when I began to bleed with Kelsi 12 weeks into my pregnancy; I kept my eyes on Him and not my situation.

When you focus on all the noise around you, you get distracted. Goal one was getting the baby here safe. Goal number two was fighting so that my husband kept his wife, and my kids kept their mother.

The Unit!

My squad was clutch. Bear with me because I am about to thank some people like I am at the Academy Awards. My husband (Kevin), my Pooh, my love, my protector was everything. He was dad, he was husband, he was nurse, he was prayer warrior, he was my safe place, he was whatever I needed so that I might focus on beating this disease. Through the process, he was probably the most affected outside of myself. Kevin, however, never wavered. He was steady. He was always upbeat. He was always optimistic and solid. He would shed a tear if it was warranted, and he would hold me tighter and ensure that no one disrupted the positive energy. I mean absolutely NO ONE. Thanks for being my knight in shining armor. Your armor is a bit dulled and chinked from all our battles, but thanks for still standing. I am thankful that God chose you for me. Pooh, thank you for always being my haven.

The blessing in all of this is that my squad was plentiful. There was my mom and dad, Patty Ann, sisters, brothers, cousins, friends, and even strangers who stepped up and loved me through this in unimaginable ways.

My magnificent mom, Katie B., was nothing short of a warrior. She was truly my ride or die. When I found out I was pregnant and had to make the tough decision she asked me point blank, "What do you want?" Weepily, I said, I want to have this baby. My mom replied,

"Then we will do everything we can to ensure that happens." At that moment, my mom was riding for me and what I wanted.

Thank you, Mom! My mom took up all the slack. She cooked, she cleaned, she loved, she laughed, she napped, she watched the kids, she watched the Young and the Restless, but most of all she never left my side. She made sure that I had no worries. Thank you for ensuring that I could just be.

Daddy, my quiet prayer warrior. My dad is always on the prayer line with Jesus. This man has awakened early every morning and read his Bible. He ensured that we saw this behavior. He ensured that God was always the constant and that we knew that. So, when I got diagnosed and then when I found out I was pregnant, maaaaaaaan, you know I told dad to direct connect God and let Him know that his baby girl needed him ASAP. He helped activate my prayer life and since I am closer to the woman at the well than the sanctified Ruth, my prayers had some cussing in it! However, God truly heard my heart. Daddy, thank you for always praying for me and ensuring that I knew about God and His awesomeness. Thank you for always being present and available.

My Patty Ann aka bonus mom aka friend. She stepped in and did whatever needed to be done to support us. She was not only the babysitter of both of our kids, but she was also the night shift when I started chemo. Patty Ann moved in and would relieve my mom, the day shift, and ensured that my home was clean and ran like a well-oiled machine. She did not have to do any of that. She has loved and cared for me as if I was an extension of her and for that, I am forever grateful.

Dee, my sister-in-love, tapped in on the weekends. Dee could have been out in her freakum dress and enjoying her life, but she sacrificed and hung out with me and her nieces. Dee, thank you!

To my first best friends, my brothers, you did like you always have and stood around me. I know it was just as hard for you to walk through this and see me in such a state but thank you for doing it. You all showed me love in your special ways. Duron, my steady, trusty, quiet protector sent random texts and did water drop-offs. Alvin always provided additional research from all the medical professionals that he encountered and gave me questions to ask. Dwayne, I know this was by far hardest for you so you went into hiding, but like a turtle when you could be strong and not be afraid, you came out to show me you were there and made me laugh. What I understand and appreciate is that you all loved me from a pure place and only wanted me to have the best, so you did your part to give me that. You all have always been there for me. More importantly, thank you to all your significant others who held you up while you all put on a brave face for me. Thank you for all they did for me because they love you and know what I mean to you. I am blessed by your love.

Then there were my peeps, specifically Rhonda, Denise, and Janet. They just got in and did whatever needed to be done. Rhonda provided child babysitting services, best friend distraction services, and just quiet, steady, and love services. She was/is a constant source of solace. She kept my medical stuff organized for me and always made me laugh. She indulged in every inappropriate joke and never missed a step.

Rocky, my sister, you have been walking lockstep with me for a long time and even carrying me when I couldn't. I am alive and healthy because of your role in my life. Denise ensured that my work affairs were cared for. She supported me most by providing homeopathic remedies and modalities during my pregnancy process because it was so important to me not to do anything that would harm my baby and ensure that she had the best chance of getting here safely. Your generosity and the way you insulated me during this process was invaluable.

Janet, thank you for being a pillar. Janet laughs at all my jokes. Janet comes in quietly and brings in quiet strength and good juju. Thank you for that calming energy and understanding.

There were strangers, acquaintances, and friends who did random acts of kindness for me. Some didn't know me except through my story on social media. There were others who we may have gone to school together and they just thought enough of me to do something to brighten my day. Thank you to all of those who donated leave, money, time, food, baby gifts, t-shirts, leggings, flowers, alkaline water drop-offs, organic juices, and prayers. All those things made me feel so much love and encouraged me.

Finally, my core Jennifer Ann and Jasmine, my Breasties. They didn't know my back story, but they were the living, breathing, embodiment of my current story. The space you two held not only during that process, but today is irreplaceable. You got me in a way that no one else can and I thank God that He made you all my first support group. Titties up to both of you.

It's not all about YOU

Everything that I have gone through in this life has been to help others not feel alone. It is to help others know that there is someone else who has been through this and is here to help. There is a non-judgmental place that wants to help you. That is why I am so transparent about my life. Honestly, at the beginning of my diagnosis, I didn't want to share it with anyone. So, I didn't. I, mouth almighty, kept it to myself. I got diagnosed in October and by January/ February I was about to burst and so I began my blog, Pregnant with a Side of Cancer (https://pregnantwithasideofcancer.wordpress.com/). I couldn't contain it anymore. I felt as if I was being poisoned or something. I was in such a twisted-up space. I had so many conflicting feelings and they had to come out. Now, I should have probably just taken them all and wrote a whole novel, but the blog satiated an immediate need to share.

From the blog, I met my first Breastie and was linked with my second. I still get emails and inboxes about helping others today and I know this is my new path and I boldly embrace it. My Breasties and I are looking to broaden our lifework so stay tuned. Monthly, we all get together and make pillows to donate to the local hospitals; it's a wonderful time. We drink, stitch, drink, laugh, drink, cry, drink, and share. You get the theme. We also provide gift bags to newly diagnosed patients who enter our tribe. Having bad titty meat sucks balls, but it is nothing like having people who truly get what you are going through walking alongside you. My goal is to ensure that no woman goes through breast cancer alone. There was no better feeling for me than knowing that I could talk to my Breasties any time of day or night to process and just share.

I am also starting a coaching business because I understand the conclusion of the cancer process doesn't conclude the emotional rollercoaster and I want us all to be the best versions of ourselves. We have so many things locked up within. There are new goals and priorities and demons to offload. I want to be the permission slip that allows you to create, cast, cut, and live out your life on your terms. One day you will no longer need permission from others. You will have the power to grant yourself permission and self-validate. That is some empowering shit, you hear me?!

My Advice

You own this journey. Your journey, although similar in diagnoses and perception, is not the same as mine or anyone else's. You have the right to make your own decisions. You are complete. You are competent. You know what is right for you. If you mess it up, it is okay. If you are still breathing at the end of it, you have a chance to do better next time. Own it, but don't let people keep you in a space that you have grown past. Detox from all things, people, and spaces that add toxicity in your life. Yep, even the ones closest to you. To battle this, you will need to be your best self. Get a squad. Even if it's just a squad of one. If you need one, then let me and/or my Breasties be that for you. No one should have to walk this alone.

John 11.4

Survivor: Dr. LaKeisha S. McGee
@specialistmcgee

Diagnosis Date:
November 7, 2018

Diagnosis:
Stage 2 Grade 7 Estrogen, Progesterone and HER2+

Age at Diagnosis: 44

Treatment Plan:
Bilateral Mastectomy
8 Lymph Nodes Removed
Port Insertion
19 Rounds of Chemotherapy
(Taxol, Perjeta, Herceptin, Carboplatin)
Breast Reconstruction/Implants
35 Rounds of Radiation

Maintenance Plan:
5 Years of Anastrozole

Birthdays have always been important to me and I spent my 45th birthday in the hospital, crying and pleading for a heating pad for my back. I was in so much pain, I was devastated, and I couldn't understand it! It was March 23, 2019, and I was on day four of my hospital admission. I had fallen asleep early that night. The medication kept me feeling sluggish. I honestly thought they were trying to prolong my stay LOL. For a minute, I started hallucinating. I was lightheaded and dizzy most of the time and all I could do was lie down. I felt like I was hearing things and even felt a presence in my room that was making me sick. Now I don't know about you, but I believe in spiritual warfare and at the time I believed I was in the middle of a battle. I knew chemo wouldn't be easy, but I never imagined it would be like that. I thought I would be better off at home than in the hospital. At least there I could be with my babies. I couldn't keep anything down or anything in. Everything irritated me physically; I was so weak. I woke up at 3:30 am. I had never questioned the father's will for my life or even said why me, but that day I was angry! Let's rewind.

My daughter, Journi, is an actress, so we decided to move to Los Angeles and allow her to pursue her acting career. It was a bold decision and a total faith walk as I would be a stranger in unknown territory and so out of my comfort zone. I left my mom; I'm her only child. I left my firstborn, who was in a detention center at the time and I was leaving my dad who was sick. Not to mention I was newly divorced, with no family in California except my estranged sister-in-law who lived at least an hour away. I also didn't have a job. I resigned from my career of 16 years. It was just my three children, Yahweh, and me. Despite my ex-husband being against the move (I understood his concerns), my parents were my biggest supporters. My middle son was my backbone. He made a selfless decision to sacrifice his senior year of college and move with us to help the girls and I transition. I was so grateful that he decided to stay with us but honestly, as a mom, I felt horrible that my life choices were impacting his.

A month after we relocated, my dad's condition worsened, and he passed from lung cancer. That was hard on us; honestly, we're still grieving. I don't know how, but somewhere along the journey, we became homeless. Somehow though, Journi was still going to all her trainings, auditions and still maintaining straight A's while we were living in our truck. Very few people knew what was going on. We stayed in hotels, Airbnb's, we rented bedrooms from a mean lady (we couldn't wait to go), and we even stayed in a shelter. Jordan had broken both his left hand and his right wrist (twice). He had to have multiple surgeries so he couldn't work. I'll never forget the day we had $4 to our name and we had to eat. Yahweh is always on time; His record is good with me. Eventually, Yahweh blessed us to get back on track with the help of the Veterans Administration. I swear, being a veteran is a blessing. That's a whole other story for another time.

That year came and went, and Jordan left to finish what he started. That left the girls and I alone to navigate our day to day lives as well as life in the entertainment industry. Juggling all those responsibilities alone was hell, but Yah! I decided to drive Uber so I could be flexible for the girls and myself. I was working on my dissertation, trying to complete my LCSW and build a network of professionals to connect with. Journi had acting classes, dance class five times a week, vocal lessons, piano lessons, auditions, and she worked on set all day when she booked. To add a cherry on top, my youngest daughter had recently been diagnosed with Autism which required a lot of time, patience, and support. I was carrying the physical and emotional load of three people and feeling guilty as heck that I had made such a big sacrifice for one of my children. It was times that I didn't feel like I was doing the greatest good for the greatest number of people. The sacrifice was great but worth it. Journi is so talented and one day she will be an EGOT winner. PeriodT.

I had to paint the picture for you so you could know how and why I ignored all the signs. My plate was running over, and I neglected to provide myself with care. Honestly, it started with a lump that I vividly remember having in my left breast in 2015. The bloody discharge and some minor discomfort that plagued me from time to time came in 2018. I didn't let the bleeding that had gone on for at least six months or the lump that had been there since at least 2015 stop me. One would think that I would've paid closer attention to it since my cousin had been diagnosed with breast cancer just a little less than two years before me. Honestly, it never crossed my mind that I would be a candidate for cancer. I'd always worked out, ran marathons, never smoked, probably had half a glass of wine a year and I didn't eat red meats or rarely consumed dairy. The crazy thing was I always got my mammogram every August since I turned forty and the doctors said I was okay. What I learned was that cancer doesn't discriminate and it doesn't play fairly. Anybody can get it; tag you can be it!

In July of 2018, I was receiving an award in Chicago and we planned on staying for the remainder of the summer. We missed our flight because I fell asleep from exhaustion and totaled my car. By the grace of Yahweh, I walked away with only a severe case of bruised ribs. You would think that I would have slowed down and got a complete checkup, but I didn't. I kept pushing. Sometimes being strong can be a weakness. A few days later, we took a flight home. When I got to Chicago, I was in so much pain that I finally paid attention to my body. I did a little research about bloody discharge from the nipple. I found three possible reasons: 1) A nursing mother…ummm NOT! 2) Infection of the nipple or 3) Cancer. I keep saying to myself I should've been more alarmed, but nope, it was summertime in Chi. After the research, I knew I had to do something, but I was home. I couldn't miss Summertime Chi; after all, I deserved it. Let me explain. There's no place like Chicago in the summer! Chicago is known for its summers, the festivals, the beaches, dancing under the stars, the hot humid weather, and the food. I was homesick and all that I had been through, I deserved to be with my village and enjoy that time.

I shared with my younger sister Sherissa, who is my confidant, what I was experiencing and after many conversations with her I heard the fear and concern in her voice, and I took them seriously. I told her once I got back to Los Angeles, I would start looking into it. I did just that. Upon my arrival home, I immediately made an appointment to see my doctor.

The day finally came, and it was time for my checkup. The doctor examined me as we discussed my mommy makeover. I was ready to turn this body around. She felt the lump and with this concerned look on her face she asked, "How long has this been there?" I replied, "2015 is what I remember." I added, "Oh yea, my nipple's been bleeding as well." As crazy as it sounds, I was so excited about the mommy makeover that I almost forgot why I was there. She decided to send me for a mammogram and set me up with a plastic surgeon.

Unfortunately, I had the plastic surgeon appointment before the mammogram. During the consultation, the plastic surgeon examined my breasts, which sparked a discussion about the lump. He was very concerned and sent me to an oncologist. To think, all I wanted was to see my "girls" full and sitting right all by themselves again like they did before I had kids. But all I saw were red flags.

I had my mammogram, ultrasound, and oncologist appointment all within two weeks. They weren't playing! When the oncologist brought me back in again, he told me he saw something but wasn't concerned. He sent me for an MRI as a precaution. When he received the MRI results, not only did he see one lump, but I had a second one. Things got real for me, real quick. I had two lumps, and the doctor wanted me to have a biopsy. Honestly, after the research that I had done, I felt in my spirit that it was cancer, so I wasn't surprised at his findings. I did know that no matter what I would be ok.

When I went for the biopsy, I was shocked I had a young, black radiologist. He was cool, deeply knowledgeable, and professional. He shared with me that his job was personal. He had lost a few loved ones to cancer and wanted to find solutions to help others. He made me feel comfortable, so I asked him to be upfront and honest with me. Against protocol and in his professional opinion, he straightforwardly told me he was 95% sure the biopsy would come back cancerous. If it didn't, he highly advised me to have the lumps removed anyway.

Five days later, on November 7, 2018, I was taking my daughter Journi on a high school tour. (Yea, I couldn't believe it either—high school!) My doctor called and said, "LaKeisha, I'm not going to have you come in for this." I thought, cool, it's not that bad. But then she said, "I'm so sorry, it's cancer. We caught it early enough to beat it!" She told me it was invasive ductal carcinoma. I froze at that moment, trying to keep it together. I think I was in shock or disbelief. I know I was nervous and immediately felt weak. I didn't want to break down in front of Journi, so after we got signed in and she was situated I ran to the bathroom to catch my breath and call my mom and my sister. I couldn't stop crying, Lord, I couldn't stop crying! I don't remember what my mom said because I was still in shock. If I remember correctly, she was calm and consoling me saying she would come to take care of me, but I think my sister started to cry. That part is a blur for me.

I called my sons. Jordan asked lots of questions and said, "Okay, I'm going to take the rest of the semester off and come take care of you." He's always my protector. Jason asked some questions, but he became silent and withdrew from me. I think it was too much for him to bear. I was his shero and he had never seen me be vulnerable in that capacity. He remained my encourager throughout the process, always texting me with words of strength and love. We talked everyday but he wouldn't come and do chemo with me. I told my daughters, Journi and Jouris, last. Journi was so strong. I didn't think she would take it as well as she did, but she showed me her strength the entire time. Jouris didn't understand but her affection for me when I was sick was agape. As the youngest, Jouris would lie on the floor with me when I couldn't get up, and my Journi helped me get dressed or in and out of the tub. My girls were so loving and supportive.

Fast forward. It was my first doctor's visit, and it was a disaster! I already felt so unsettled. My girlfriend Selena took off work to go with me and after waiting for over an hour, the staff came out and had the nerves to tell us I had to reschedule. Oh boy, I was on fire! How rude to tell a patient who is waiting with anticipation to get the worse news of her life to reschedule. That experience made me so uncomfortable that I called my provider to switch doctors. I couldn't go back there; my level of comfort was broken.

I was on pins and needles as another two weeks went by, but finally, it was the day. That appointment was much better. The staff was nice and friendly, and I only waited ten minutes. The two experiences were like night and day. The doctor seemed empathetic, and although he was young, he assured me he would do his best to make it easy for me. He was patient, answered all my questions, and even gave me his personal cell phone number. The original diagnosis was invasive ductal carcinoma, but after the pathology report, I was diagnosed with Stage 2 Grade 7 HER2+ ER+ PR+. I was triple positive. The diagnosis was worse but the treatment options to fight it were better than other kinds of breast cancer. I was grateful because it could've been so much worse due to my negligence of self-care. I've learned a valuable lesson the hard way about making me last. I still had a fighting chance. I was ignorant, of course, and didn't have a clue what it all meant, but the doctor gave me so many materials to read that I would know. I was overwhelmed.

The suggested treatment plan was to have a unilateral mastectomy, 19 rounds of chemo, and 35 rounds of radiation. Wow, wow, wow! I agreed with everything except I wanted a new pair of boobs out of the deal! I also requested the double mastectomy to lessen the chances of cancer coming back, but I didn't know that's not how it works completely. Next, I met the surgical oncologist, and he wanted to do the surgery as soon as possible in December, but I wanted a plastic surgeon in the room to start my reconstruction. I soon found out when you have state insurance, your options are limited. The insurance gave me a list of four doctors. With my limited options, I started the research.

Yahweh is so good! The doctor I wanted worked out of Orange County but because I serve a good Yahweh, he had hospital privileges to work out of the hospital in Los Angeles County with my surgical oncologist. The only problem was that he was booked until January 31, 2019, almost three months after my diagnosis. My oncologist advised me against prolonging the surgery. He said it was possible it could spread going, from stage 2 to stage 3, but I was steadfast and unmovable. I changed my diet, went completely plant-based and eliminated all sweets. After my surgery, my doctor told me my tumors had shrunk. I think it was due to the diet changes.

On January 31, 2019, I had a bilateral mastectomy and eight lymph nodes removed from my left arm. I was surrounded by amazing support: my beautiful mother (who took the year off work to care for me), my children, my sister, my cousin, my sorors (ships) and my LA friends. Being a native of Chicago, I was so blessed to have loved ones fly to Los Angeles to be with me. I was ready to fight!

All went well with the surgery, but I woke up itching with four drain bottles attached to my body. The doctor thought it was just the anesthesia, but I had an allergic reaction to the ChloraPrep. I had broken out all over my torso and face, and it was unbearable. I couldn't focus on the pain or my healing because I was itching so badly. That reaction gave me an extra five-day hospital stay. I was finally released, but the allergic reaction got worse before it got better. Man, I tell you what an awful six to eight weeks that I was miserable. I left the hospital with my expanders in and they had been expanded some. I started going to the plastic surgeon three weeks after surgery for my first tissue expansion. That process was to stretch and expand my breast tissue for the implants. I went every three weeks for a few months. That wasn't bad; it only hurt when the doctor inserted the needle into my breast at first. However, the more the doctor expanded, the tighter my breast got, and the more pressure built up it felt like my breast would explode.

Two weeks after my first expansion it was time to have my port put in. All went well, but it took some getting used to. It felt weird like something was obstructing my neck and throat keeping me from moving and turning my head which caused soreness in my neck and throat. It also felt like something was pulling at my heart.

I started chemo on March 15, 2019. I was nervous as hell. The first day was eight hours. I took four different chemo drugs: Taxol, Perjeta, Herceptin, and Carboplatin. When it was over, I felt some relief because I did it, but I felt a whole lot of anxiety waiting on the unknown. By the time I started to head home, I was so sick I couldn't keep anything in or down. The next day, I was so weak I could barely walk. I had to go back and get a shot called Fulphia or Zarxio. This shot is given 1-3 days after chemo to help stimulate your bone marrow to produce white blood cells. The shot hurt so bad that I felt like I was in labor for three days at a time. I spent the next two to three days in the bathroom. My stomach and back would cramp so badly; I spent hours in the tub for relief.

I couldn't keep anything down, causing me to experience severe dehydration. I went to the cancer center for hydration, but that didn't work. My sissy, Meako, flew in town to cut my hair before chemo started to take it out. I wanted to control something. Well, this led to my birthday, where I ended up in the hospital. I had diarrhea so bad, I had gone to the bathroom 33 times within 24 hours. It was crazy! The doctors hospitalized me, which brings us back to the beginning of my story.

Throughout my journey, I was subjected to so much. My nails turned black, I was extremely lethargic all the time, my hair fell out, my vagina felt like I had a bladder infection constantly, my eye turned pink and I had to wear an eye cover because I couldn't see. My once perfect, 20/20 vision had been damaged and I started seeing blurs. Before cancer, I was diagnosed with vertigo which caused frequent migraines. Those migraines intensified tremendously as I was going through my treatments. My legs got so heavy I could barely walk; it was due to nerve damage neuropathy. My baby would rub them down every night. My hands and toes would ache and lock up sending shooting severe pains throughout my nervous system due to neuropathy. My back hurt so bad that I couldn't get up and my memory was foggy, so I'd forget my thoughts mid-sentence. My mouth had sores inside; my left arm remains numb and aches to this very day. I can't lift more than five pounds on it and according to the doctor, I will never be able to lift more than that. I must wear a sleeve on it to prevent swelling.

I'm now completely in full-fledged menopause. This hurt me not because I planned on having more children, but because my choice was taken away from me. As a woman, one of our jobs is to bring forth life and even though I already had four children, I was so hurt that I couldn't produce any more without having to do IVF or some other procedure. I cried like a baby because I loved being pregnant. It's so beautiful. Yahweh put us here to reproduce and I felt insecure, less than a woman. The women in my family had babies late and, to my knowledge, I'm the only one who went through menopause early. I've never been one to have perspiration but now I have extremely bad hot flashes where I wake up soaking wet. Sleep doesn't live here anymore!

Every week I had to have my blood drawn to make sure my white blood count was high enough for me to continue treatment. A few times it was so low that I had to miss chemo for eight weeks. I also had to have the Zarxio shot for ten days straight. As I said, imagine being in active labor for ten days straight, that's what it felt like.

After being diagnosed with the same breast cancer as my cousin, I thought it was important to get tested for the Breast Cancer Gene

(BRCA) which came back negative. On my mother's paternal side, we have had several family members to be affected by and die from cancer. Three out of four siblings had some form of cancer, three passed from it. Three out of those four siblings had children to be affected by some form of cancer and two passed. Then there was me, the granddaughter of one of those siblings, affected by breast cancer. I began to think that we were affected by a cancer gene.

When I was diagnosed with cancer, I had no idea what to expect, but my village support was so strong. I don't think anyone cried except maybe one or two people. My mom is the true shero. What strength, courage, and selflessness she shows me. Mommy (Darlene) came and took care of me. Without her, I wouldn't have made it. She became me! She drove the girls everywhere and waited for them, cooked them dinner and took them to school. She helped me out the tub, all after having her knee replacement surgery. Thank you, Mom. At some point my mother had to take care of my grandfather who was also diagnosed with cancer. Mr. Arthur H. Ross fought a good fight but went home to be with the Lord.

My friends and family stepped up too. They came, they sent, they paid, they supported, and I'm so grateful. My village went to chemo with me just to sit and hold my hand. I tell you, I was blessed. I even watched strangers show up for me with the love of Yahweh. People that I didn't know would donate money or send me care packages to help me along the way. No one has to be nice to you. It's just a blessing for me that throughout my process people were. I'm forever humbled.

Yahweh assured me that I would be ok no matter what. There were days I couldn't pray for myself. There were days that I was so depressed I couldn't get out of bed, but I kept waking up and I kept believing. I kept trusting that Yahweh had better plans for my life and that this was just a test. See, I believe in the power of healing and how it's going to change our communities. Yahweh had to give me physical healing so I could relate to that population of his people that needed such a testimony as mine.

I've completed two reconstruction surgeries, 35 rounds of radiation and 19 rounds of chemo. Ironically, I took my last round on

March 16, 2020, almost a year to the date of my first one. I was finished four days before my birthday and thanks to COVID-19, I was still on quarantine and didn't get to celebrate yet another birthday the way I wanted. LOL No complaints though. I'm cancer free! No skin was broken, and my breast remained intact after all that. Thank Yahweh! I had two surgeries to put in and take out the port. I have one possible surgery left to finish up my breast reconstruction which may include a fat graph. I'm required to take an echocardiogram every three months to check my heart function and PET and CT scans every three to six months to check and make sure the cancer hasn't returned for the first year. By the grace of Yahweh, mine have all come back clean.

My maintenance plan includes taking Anastrozole for five years. Normally, women are given Tamoxifen, but I've already completed menopause so that's not an option for me. I'm going to need to do some physical therapy for my arm and I pray that the neuropathy reverses as much as possible. As of now, I still experience weakness in my legs and severe aches and pains in my back, hands, and feet. It feels like severe Charlie horses and arthritis mixed. My vision is still blurry sometimes and I'm still very lethargic. I'm under the care of a neurologist because my arm is still numb, and I still get a foggy brain and forget things. I know I make this thing look easy, but it's not at all. I'm just determined to win!

On March 23, 2019, at 3:00 am when I woke up mad as hell because I was spending my birthday in the hospital, Yahweh gave me hope, peace, strength, and courage to fight this thing. He reminded me that I was an heir to the throne and that the same principles of healing, joy, and life were mine if I just believed. I knew no matter what, my test was a part of my testimony and that I would be healed because healing is my portion.

Yahweh gave me a personal charge and responsibility to create a platform to talk about breast cancer, awareness, early detection, and solutions for others. The Bible says, "he'll use the least of us" and in the middle of treatment Yahweh did exactly that. He used me to show others courage and that if you believe, anything is possible! On October 18, 2019, I became a model for cabionline.com. I left radiation and went directly to the set. I don't look like what I've been through; check out the campaign and you'll see Yahweh's hands all over me. His grace and mercy are sufficient for me. I also became a speaker for Susan G. Komen. I started going to events sharing my experience and knowledge about breast cancer. Yahweh allowed me to finish my Ph.D. and still be able to be my daughter's momager. Now, this didn't happen all at once and of course, a lot of it took place from my bed, but I took advantage of the good days. I forced myself to get up and go even if that meant I slept in the car when she went into her appointments.

Yahweh allowed my son to graduate from college and my baby to become more independent and stable with understanding Autism. Yahweh told me to write an anthology and to create a foundation to help other survivors through the hardest chapters of their healing process. Heal Her2 Foundation is up and running. It's the place where we believe healing is the new normal. By the power of Yahweh and through the teachings of Metanoia, we will heal one person at a time.

My advice is to go get tested. Early detection saves lives. Don't do like I did and put it off. Yahweh spared me! If you find yourself walking in my shoes, keep believing, take it one day at a time, surround yourself with positive people and things and be grateful. Most of all, dig deep down inside and look for that healthy, happy place. Go there and don't come back until you have healed. *Shalom.*

Not just surviving, thriving.

Beauty & The Beast

Survivor: Kenya Johnson-Brown

Diagnosis Date: December 2018

Diagnosis:
Stage 1B Triple Negative

Age at Diagnosis: 47

Treatment Plan:
Lumpectomy
6 Lymph Nodes Removed
Port Insertion
8 Rounds of Chemotherapy
(Doxorubicin, Taxotere, Cyclophosphamide)
38 Rounds of Radiation

In November of 2018, I felt a few knots in my right breast that would have been alarming to someone else, but I ignored the signs, got dressed and proceeded to do what I set out to do for that day. I spoke to my sister telling her about it and she responded, "Girl, when was the last time you had a mammogram?" I replied, "Girl, I haven't ever had a mammogram. She said, "Hang up from me now and call your doctor to make an appointment." I did just that and my doctor set me up to have a mammogram completed in December of 2018, which was three weeks later. I learned a valuable lesson—never to go get a test like that done by yourself. Nevertheless, the technician called my name and we walked back to the room where the procedure took place. She explained how the procedure would go. Once the procedure was over,

I was asked to get dressed and head back to the waiting room and wait for my name to be called again. The doctor had to go over the results just in case they needed to take more photos. If the photos came out great, then I would be able to go home.

I was in the waiting room jumping to 217 different conclusions as to why she was taking so long to come back and tell me something. That's when I learned why I needed someone with me. It's so important to have someone with you so they can keep you distracted. As I continued to wait, I developed an extreme migraine headache. Then, the technician finally told me that the doctor needed more photos. My anxiety kicked in at full speed. As she was taking more photos, another tech came in with the doctor and started asking me a lot of questions. My heart instantly dropped into my stomach and down to the floor. At that point, I came to my conclusion that I officially had breast cancer. I was on the table crying internally, saying *"Why me, Lord? I have been on this cruise ship for seven years with no end destination. Oh Lord, please help me."*

In 2012, I was diagnosed with chronic depression. In 2013, I contracted the West Nile Virus and still currently have a balloon in my head and will for the rest of my life. In 2014, I was kidnapped and held captive for two days for ransom money. Then in 2015, I was diagnosed with post-traumatic stress disorder. In 2016, I got a divorce. Then came The Big C! In December of 2018, I was officially diagnosed with breast cancer.

I snapped back from thoughts as they told me that I needed an emergency ultrasound. I was hysterical. I began asking questions. "Why? What is it? Do you all see something?" The doctor responded, "Miss Johnson, please try to relax and don't jump to conclusions because we have to complete several different steps before we give your doctor your prognosis." I was lying there about to have a nervous breakdown from worrying when I received a text that said, "Kenya, the doctor is requesting a biopsy."

That's when I lost it. I was yelling. "So, you are still telling me I should relax? No way, Jose! I'm not crazy. Something's not right. Ain't nothing good about this, doctor. Please tell me because both of my grandmothers passed away from cancer and my father passed away from prostate cancer. So, I am at a high risk to contract this disease." The doctor calmly responded, "I'm going to enter the test results and your doctor will be contacting you with the results within three business days." I couldn't believe what I was hearing. It was only Thursday and I would have to wait until the next week to get my results. My mind began to race. *This is unacceptable behavior and I cannot process this b******* that they are doing! This can't be legal. I can't believe they think I can go on for the next couple of days like business-as-usual. That's not possible. These people need to think logically. Can't they see I'm panicking? Now, I can barely breathe.*

I made it longer than I thought I could. I was officially on my third day of awaiting results and I was on pins and needles. I still could barely breathe as I anticipated that phone call from my doctor. The phone finally rang, and it was the doctor's office. The nurse navigator asked if I could come in that day to talk to the doctor about my mammogram, ultrasound, and biopsy. I said, "Yes, what day would you like me to schedule my appointment with the---" Before I could finish my question, she interrupted letting me know that would not be necessary. "I need you to be here in an hour; I want to squeeze you in." That statement let me know that the outcome would not be good. I immediately got off the phone and called my sisters, Felicia, and Gandy, and asked them to meet me at the doctor's office because my results were back.

As I drove to the doctor's office by myself, I was very numb like I was in the Twilight Zone. I arrived and had butterflies in my stomach. I sat in the car for about five minutes trying to calm down. I finally pushed myself to get out of the car and I saw both of my sisters pulling up at the same time. So, I waited anxiously for them to find parking spaces and rush in so that we would not be late. As we all approached the door, my sister Felicia said, "You all stop. Wait a minute; let's pray first because the devil is a lie." Felicia proceeded to pray and then Gandy started to intercede on my behalf as well. She asked God for favor upon favor. As we sat in the waiting room for my name to be called, I started singing *I Speak Life* by Donald Lawrence. At one point, I was so loud in the clinic that people started looking at me like I was crazy. The nurse called me and all of us stared back and forth at each other. I got up and my sister Gandy grabbed my hand. Her words still stick with me today. She said, "Don't worry. We got this." That word *we* resonated with me.

The nurse was in the back trying to make small talk as we waited for the doctor to come in, but I was too impatient to even try to engage in a conversation with her. Finally, she finished her conversation and let us know that the doctor would be in shortly. Dr. Marvella entered and, unlike her nurse, cut straight to the point. "As you know, they performed different tests to make sure that the official report was accurate. And I'm so sorry, honey, it is breast cancer." My entire body went numb and I gazed blankly at the wall. Both of my sisters started asking her a lot of questions that she could not answer. Gandy was perplexed at how she could be my doctor and not know the answers to their questions. To her concern, Dr. Marvella replied, "Yes, I am her doctor and I have been her doctor for 27 years, but that is not my expertise. Annabelle, who is the nurse navigator, has set her up with an oncologist. The oncologist, Dr. Thomas, will know what steps and procedures she needs to take. He will also let her know what stage cancer she is in."

Baffled from the doctor's response, I just sat there hearing her but not hearing her; everything was so fuzzy. As we left the office, my mind felt like a deflated football. My sisters were talking to me, but I was so stuck that I couldn't respond. Honestly, I don't even think I was able to comprehend what they said. All I heard was, *blah blah blah blah blah blah blah*. While I drove home, both kept calling me to ask if I was okay and I repeatedly told them yes. Gandy said, "Nikki, it's okay to be afraid. You don't have to be strong all the time. We know that you are used to being in control of everything and now you are not because you have to comply with this shocking news you just received." Felicia got choked up and I could hear in her voice that she had been crying and freaking out. I reassured her that I was going to figure it out. I finally made it home and I stayed in the car as I called my oldest son, George, and my baby son, Donnie, on a three-way call. I explained that the test results did not come back in my favor and I had breast cancer. George and Donnie immediately started asking me a lot of questions that I couldn't answer. Both said, "Mom, don't worry about it. We got this!" Next, I called my little queen, Jakeya, who I call Jo Ann Robinson. When she heard the news, she answered, "No, Mom. That can't be possible! I just lost my dad to cancer, now you." I quickly responded with, "The devil is a lie! I ain't going nowhere. I wasn't built to break. You just focus on school and I got this."

Once I shared the devastating news with my children, I called my husband, Willie, back. I didn't even realize that I had missed his call. As soon as I picked up, he started yelling. "What is going on? Why you ain't answer your phone? What did the doctor say?" I broke the news gently. "Honey, it is possible that I do have breast cancer." After I explained that I would see an oncologist next, his response was like everyone else's. He reassured me that everything would be okay. He said, "We got this, baby. I don't need you to start panicking. Take a deep breath for me please."

With my husband and children's blessings, I was finally ready to get out of the car, but my phone would not stop ringing. My emotional sister, Felicia, had called and rallied up the troops asking them to pray for me because the results did not come back in my favor. The phone calls wouldn't stop coming so I just cut my phone off so I could sit back and have a one-on-one conversation with my heavenly father. I grabbed my Bible and went downstairs in the basement. I went straight to *Isaiah 41:10* and *Exodus 15:2*. I pondered on a few songs to keep in my belly as I walked through my journey. *I Speak Life, Seasons, God Favored Me* and *When Sunday Comes* were among my favorites. When I was finished up with my quiet time, I went upstairs to my bedroom. My husband was trying to talk to me, but my mind was consumed with my situation. My focus was to get on my laptop and scour the internet researching everything and anything related to breast cancer. At that point, I had been up for three consecutive days going from my laptop to my tablet to my phone running myself bonkers. I had taken so many notes that I had gone through a composition book. That was the worst mistake that I could have ever made. It made me more scared and more discombobulated, so please take it from me and stay away from the internet until you talk to your oncologist.

I grabbed another notebook specifically to write down questions that were significant to ask the oncologist. *What is the survival rate? Is my cancer curable or incurable? Will I need chemo? Will I need radiation! What are the different side effects if I choose to do either one? What stage of cancer is it? Maybe I need to get a second opinion. If I decide to take chemo or radiation, what would I need to expect? What are the chances of the cancer recurrence? Would I need to have surgery and if so, explain the type of surgery and why the surgery is needed? Is the cancer aggressive?* I had so many questions and I was intentional about getting answers to all of them. I remembered that lesson from school that no question is a stupid question.

The day arrived where I could finally take a breath because it was time to see my oncologist. I had so much support that day. My husband, my daughter, both of my sons, my sisters, and my biggest cheerleaders—Tensi, Sherita, Tangie, Sarah, and Deborah were all there with me. My Aunt Aqua was also there. She has always been like a mother to my sisters and me. The doctor came in and introduced himself and told me that I had a tumor in my right breast that needed to come out immediately. He told us that it was Stage 1B Triple Negative. Dr. Thomas was adamant about the urgency of scheduling my surgery immediately. He was overly concerned because the cancer was very aggressive. I pulled out my book with my long list of questions. Dr. Thomas excused himself and came back with a chair to sit down so he could answer my questions. He was thorough and patient as he addressed all my concerns. He even asked my family if they had any questions. Of course, they did, and Dr. Thomas was very upfront and answered them significantly.

Once our Q&A period was done, Dr. Thomas asked my family to leave the examination room so he could physically examine me so he could feel how big the lump was. When I was finished there, my husband and I headed to the surgeon's office. Dr. Bhatti completed her examination of me and told me that she already scheduled me for surgery on February 6, 2019. That was only nine days away and that just showed me that God was already in the midst. I just started yelling, "Thank You, Lord! Thank You, Lord! Thank You, Lord!" because things could have been much worse. Dr. Bhatti was looking at me like I was crazy because I started singing *Gracefully Broken*. I looked her straight in her eyes and said, "Dr. Bhatti, I'm not crazy. I'm just thanking God in advance because He has healed and delivered me."

It was 6:15 in the morning on surgery day and we were all sitting in the surgical waiting room waiting for the doctor to call my name. My squad was present for comfort and support. Once I was out of surgery and in the recovery room and my support system was so overwhelming. There were so many people there to greet me. The doctor came in to give me an update on how the procedure went. She informed me that everything went well. She removed the tumor, which was much bigger than she expected. Dr. Bhatti also removed some of my lymph nodes from under my arm. I was so grateful when she shared that they were tested and came back negative for cancer. *Thank You, Lord! You have done it again!*

When it was time to be discharged from the hospital, I was given a folder with valuable information regarding the necessary things I needed to do after the surgery and the main things that I couldn't do. I was especially restricted from lifting anything over ten pounds on my right side. Some of the items that I needed after surgery were sports bras, organic soap or soap with no fragrance, white washcloths (no dye), and A&D Ointment to apply to my scars. I was instructed to get plenty of rest and take my pain meds as prescribed. Also, before I was released from the hospital, I already had scheduled my appointment to go in for surgery to get my port in. Everyone doesn't get a port, but I chose to so that it would be easy access and they don't have to keep poking me to administer the chemotherapy.

February 24th was the date that I went in for my port insertion. My sister, Felicia and my son, Donnie were with me. The surgery went well and besides a little drowsiness from the medication, I did not experience any side effects. My first day of chemo was scheduled for March 6th. That morning I had been on the phone with family members and friends since 4 a.m. with everyone repeating the same thing: "Don't worry; everything is going to be okay. We all are going to be right there with you." I started the day with a healthy breakfast because I was not sure if I would want anything to eat after the chemo. It was hard to eat because I was nervous and anticipating that day for weeks. I dressed comfortably and made sure to grab my pillow, blanket, and a few bottles of water.

Felicia and Gandy traveled with me to the clinic that morning and a few of my close friends were going to meet us there. My sister prepared a feast at home for about 30 to 40 people. She had sub sandwiches, veggie and fruit trays, water, pop, and juice. She also made me a two-tier breast cancer cake.

I sat down and the nurse checked my wristband and asked my name and my birthday. She explained how the procedure would go. The first drugs she hooked up were the pre-med steroids, anti-anxiety, anti-nausea, and finally a saline solution. When the meds were finished, the machine started beeping and making an annoying noise letting the nurse and everyone else know that it was finished. I wasn't sure if I was just nervous, but it seemed like I could feel every infusion going through my body. Next, it was time to start with the Red Devil first (Doxorubicin). Then, I received Taxotere which is the bold one. Lastly, I had Mr. Toxic (Cyclophosphamide).

The first day of chemo was very draining. When I got home, there were a lot of family members there to greet me. Everybody asked how I was feeling, and I was honest when I said that I felt okay. Nothing had kicked in yet. Around 7:00 pm, everyone started leaving and I went upstairs to rest. I woke up at about 1:00 am feeling horrible. My body was all out of whack and I was very nauseous and very fatigued. I instantly woke my husband up and told him how I felt. He jumped up to get me water and my nausea pills. I learned that day not to wait until I felt ill to take the nausea medication. I began to feel a little better, but by 4:00 am, the nausea returned. I told my husband to call my sister over immediately. They both lived twenty minutes from me and arrived at my house at about 4:30 am. By the time they got upstairs, I was on the floor with strange reactions. My daughter and sisters rubbed my back, leg, and arm. I tried to get back in the bed but that didn't work. My sister tried to put me in the tub thinking it would make me feel better, but it only seemed to make me feel worse. No one told me that I would have those kinds of reactions from the chemo. I was on the bathroom floor crying, asking God to please help me. My daughter was asking me what was wrong, but I didn't have the answer.

I told her to call the ambulance because something was not right. My husband told my son to start the car so he could take me to the emergency room, but I insisted that they call 9-1-1. However, my husband and son carried me to the car and drove me to the emergency room. When we arrived, I was unresponsive, and the medical professionals had to revive me. This is rare, but it can happen, and it landed me in the ICU for three days before I was transferred to a regular room for two more days. My oncologist was surprised because that was my first chemo treatment. That treatment knocked me down to where I needed to go home with a nurse two times a week and physical therapy and occupational therapy three times a week because I could barely walk. The doctor decreased the amount of chemo meds that I received, which added more time to the overall treatment, but I didn't care. I couldn't take that reaction again. So, instead of four more treatments left every 21 days, I ended up having seven more treatments every 21 days.

I lost all my hair on the first round of chemo and my sister, Felicia, started making my wigs. I also had to learn how to stylishly tie and wear scarves on my head. What was so amusing to me is when my hair started to grow back, it grew like a little troll. I had hair in the middle and some in the back. That's not actually what I had in mind when I said I wanted a mohawk! I learned that you would lose all the hair on your body as a result of chemo. I had to learn how to draw my eyebrows on!

Alas! The day came for my chemo to end. On July 18, 2019, I was officially done! *Hallelujah! Thank you, Lord! I made it!*

Here is a list of some of the things that I experienced during chemo that you may need to be aware of:

1. You will not have an appetite, but make sure you eat something.
2. You will get mouth sores, but don't worry they will give you medication for that.
3. Some days you won't be able to even get out of bed.
4. Some days you won't be able to even walk.
5. Your bones will ache so badly.

6. Your fingernails will turn black and crack and start to even peel off.
7. You will experience hot flashes, diarrhea, dry mouth, and be very fatigued.
8. Your back will itch so bad.
9. You will get numbness in your hands, feet, legs, and sometimes your arms.
10. Your eyeballs will hurt as if they are about to pop out your head.
11. Your balance will be off.
12. You will get something called neuropathy, which is an intense and sharp numbing pain that won't let up.
13. You may experience inflammatory arthritis, which they failed to mention to me.
14. You must have gloves and plenty of Lysol spray and wipes.

While taking chemo, your doctor will stress some things that you need to do:

1. Exercise even when you don't feel like it
2. Drink plenty of water
3. Eat lots of fresh green vegetables fresh (no can)
4. Eat lots of fresh fruit
5. Take B12 vitamins and D3 for your immune system and your bones
6. Used Arnicare Gel for pain relief
7. Take turmeric powder or pills

On August 5, 2019, I was nervous as I spoke with Dr. Seshugirrioa, the radiation oncologist, for the first time. Of course, my sister was with me at that session where we discussed the different procedures and how many radiation treatments I would need. They also explained exactly where they needed to aim the beam to destroy all the cancer cells. I needed a total of 38 rounds of radiation treatments. The first 33 would be normal and the last five more intense. As I stood in the room where the procedure would take place, the doctors took photos and made tattoo marks on my right breast with a sharpie marker identifying exactly where to aim the beam. The tattoos are permanent, but nobody initially informed me of that.

However, at that point, you could barely see the ink and I didn't care anyway. I just wanted them to do whatever they needed to do to save my life.

At 3:42 pm on Friday, August 9th, I received a phone call from Maria, who was the clerk in the radiation department. Maria informed me that my insurance company, Illinicare, refused to cover my radiation treatment at 100%. They were only willing to pay 70% and I would need to pay the other 30% out-of-pocket, which equaled $10,000. I was very pissed that she called me at the last minute. It was near the close of business on Friday afternoon and I was scheduled to start my treatments that following Monday. I began taking every word that came out of her mouth personally. I just could not understand how she had just gotten that information; someone had seriously dropped the ball. All I knew was that they would see me on Monday morning, so it was up to them to take accountability and figure it out. I was over it because I had already endured so much with the chemo treatments. Still upset and shocked, I arrived at the radiation center on Monday to talk to someone about this situation. Overcome with emotion, I stopped talking to Maria and my sister took over the conversation. Maria gave her financial aid papers to complete and Maria walked them right to the Director of Finance, Marianne. Maria came back and told me that Marianne would push my paperwork through, but she couldn't guarantee that I would get a donor right away. However, she did call over to the radiation department to let them know to go ahead and start my radiation immediately since I had already missed out due to a lack of payment. I was so excited; all I could say was, *Thank You, Lord! Thank You, Lord! Thank You, Lord!*

My first official day of radiation was August 14, 2019. I was scheduled to go every day for 15 minutes. When I checked in, I was asked to undress from the waist up and put on my gown then go directly to the room. I entered the room feeling nervous because I was unsure of what to expect. The tech asked me to relax as she shifted my body around the table using the sheet. I was shaken when I saw that big piece of equipment coming towards me with lights on it. The machine started clicking and buzzing which made me nervous. A few short moments later, the tech came back into the room and told me that everything went well and that she would see me the next day. Radiation wasn't so bad. There was no pain from the treatment itself, but I did feel fatigued sometimes. Some days it was hard to function because the radiation had me so tired to the point that I didn't even want to get up in the morning. It seemed as if all I did was sleep. Honestly, that is all I wanted to do some days because I felt so unattractive and I just looked ugly to myself.

I started noticing that my skin was peeling. That's one of the side effects of the radiation. I had to make sure to keep some A&D Ointment and Aquaphor handy to provide relief for my cracked skin, which sometimes burned. I had to learn not to beat myself up so badly because of the way I looked. The thought of the way I physically looked before the trauma was so far from the way I viewed myself as I was going through my treatments. I learned how to do my makeup so that I could look at myself in the mirror daily. For several weeks, I couldn't even look at myself. I just could not handle it. It was just too dramatic for me. Going from beauty to the beast was a traumatizing occurrence. Who wouldn't have a meltdown? It was emotionally draining. Not only did the chemicals change my body physically, but my sex drive was all out of whack.

My treatment ended on September 20, 2019, and I am now cancer-free! Yes, I am a survivor! I crossed the finish line and I still have my vision. That was the most emotional experience I had endured in life. I am no longer powerless. This was a horrible experience but changed my life because I learned I'm much stronger than I thought. The best part of it is that I can help others through my story. Currently, I participate in organizations that bring awareness to breast cancer. I still go to the cancer center and give out survivor bags with all kinds of goodies. I participate in walks to raise awareness and funds for research. Each month, I faithfully attend the support group.

My advice to the ladies is please do your self-exam daily for nipple discharge, nipple irritation or knots in your breast. Most importantly, get your mammogram screening completed before you turn 30 years old. Early detection can save your life.

No one fights alone.

Lessons

Survivor: Andrea Simmons

Diagnosis Date:
June 4, 2019

Diagnosis:
Stage 1 Invasive Ductal Carcinoma

Age at Diagnosis: 47

Treatment Plan:
Lumpectomy
8 Lymph Nodes Removed
2 Rounds of Chemotherapy
(Adriamycin/Cytoxan and Taxol)
20 Rounds of Radiation

7/17/71—the day I was born. I'm always excited to share this date because it always sparks a conversation. "All sevens you must be lucky," or "What a great birthday!" Biblically speaking, the number seven represents divine perfection and completeness. Ironically, I've felt like damaged goods. My body has been attacked and violated by cancer, specifically breast cancer, known as Invasive Ductal Carcinoma. On June 4, 2019, I received the phone call that would forever change the course of my life. Hearing those words from the nurse on the other end of the phone made my world stop. At that moment, I had an out of body experience, envisioning myself falling down a black hole. I zoned out and was struck speechless.

How could this be? I had a mammogram in November, seven months ago and the results were negative. This gotta be a mistake! I feel perfectly fine; I do not look like a person with cancer.

Like most wives and mothers, going to the doctor was not a priority, but in 2018 I decided that I was going to be intentional about my health. Hubby and I were going to be empty nesters soon, so I had big plans for us, and I wanted to be at my best. I made doctors' appointments, got physicals, had overdue dental work done and got a mammogram. I was so proud of myself and felt so accomplished for following through and not canceling my appointments as I had done in the past. I was in control and it felt good to put myself first.

One spring evening while watching T.V., I felt a sensation in the middle of my chest equivalent to that of having an allergic reaction. I looked down and my skin was red, but by the next day the redness was gone, and everything looked normal. Throughout the week, something in my spirit compelled me to touch that area of my chest until one day I felt a small bump. I thought maybe it was a bug bite, which was odd because I had not been out that day. After a couple of days, I couldn't see anything on my skin, but I could still feel a hard bump underneath. *By this time surely a bug bite should be gone by now, right?* It dawned on me that I should probably pay close attention to it. I shared with my husband that I had a bug bite that just wouldn't go away. He also felt the bump and urged me to get it checked out as soon as possible. I was not feeling the thought of the potential out of pocket expense to see the doctor for a bug bite.

So nope, nada, not doing it, ain't gonna happen! I feel fine, the redness is gone, it's not bothering me so I'm not going to mess with it and have no doctor poking around. That was my thought process, despite pledging to be intentional about my health. *Get it together, Boo!*

I was born with an incredible sense of discernment, so in most situations, I tend to follow my gut. Within a few days, there was no escaping my intuition; the bump was still there. I needed to take my butt to the doctor.

At the doctor's, I explained to her what had been going on. Confidently, I told her that I'm sure it's nothing with my breast because I just had a mammogram a few months ago, plus the bump was near the center of my chest and nowhere near my boob. Dr. Hamilton just sat there and listened, letting me get it all out. When I was done, she said, "Well, the area you pointed out to me actually *is* a part of your breast tissue." During her examination, she said that she thought it was a cyst that commonly occurs in women. Since I had a mammogram not too long ago, she wanted to send me for a diagnostic mammogram. She explained, "You have dense breast tissue so the diagnostic mammogram will be able to see through the dense tissue to detect any issues that a regular mammogram otherwise would not be able to detect." Then she hit me with, "In the meantime, avoid caffeine." *What say what now?*

On the day of the scheduled diagnostic mammogram, Hubby went with me to the appointment. Neither one of us was overly concerned but because of what I had learned from Dr. Hamilton, he wanted to be there for support. I wasn't sure what to expect at that appointment, but I *assumed* that it was going to be as simple as getting a regular mammogram. Pull the boob out, lay it on the metal plate, boob smashed, hold your breath, take the picture and done. Wham, bam, thank ya, ma'am! Bye Felicia!

Well, it didn't go that way at all. You know what they say about you when you *assume*, right? The diagnostic mammogram was intended to not only see through the dense breast tissue in my actual boob but to also capture an image of the bump itself near the middle of my chest. However, the technician was unable to capture an image of the bump, so she had to perform an ultrasound instead. Once the technician was done, she went to get the doctor to review the ultrasound. As the doctor was looking at the monitor, she went over my chest area with the ultrasound wand. She made small talk, asked me questions about how I found the bump, was I experiencing any pain, things like that. Once she was done, she let me know that she saw a very small mass but didn't want to issue a diagnosis until more testing was done. She needed to send me for a biopsy. I could sense that she was choosing her words carefully. But as much as she tried, her facial expressions and body language spoke volumes, and it was all I needed to see. I became nervous and highly concerned.

Long ago, my husband Martin and I chose to practice a more positive way of thinking. We are glass half full type of folks. We break down the worst-case scenario in any situation and discuss the possibilities for the worst that can happen, and how can we deal with them. What are the take-a-ways, and what can we learn from them to do better and be better? However, in this situation when the worst-case scenario of having breast cancer is as ominous as death, how do you reconcile with that?!

The car ride home seemed like forever. I cried while my husband put his best effort into being optimistic, but his facial expressions said it all. I knew he was worried. His mother had passed away from an illness when he and his siblings were teenagers, so I knew that's what was on his mind. We decided to not share all the details of the appointment with the girls and just tell them that I needed to get more testing done. We certainly were not going to mention the "c-word" and have that upset their world prematurely.

The Charlotte Radiology team was great about getting me an appointment for the biopsy within a relatively short amount of time. Within a week or so we were at Atrium Hospital. I was grateful because I knew that anything longer than that would have been unbearable for me. The sooner we got it done, the sooner we got answers. Days leading up to the day, I was anxious about the procedure. I didn't know much about what was about to go down, so I, of course, Googled it. Bad idea. Searching the internet will have you thinking that you only have three months to live and you'll get lost down the rabbit hole.

The nurse came to prep me for the procedure and explained thoroughly what I should expect. While waiting for the numbing medicine to take effect, she took me into another room to run a diagnostic mammogram. However, just like before, she was unable to do so due to the location of the mass being near the middle of my chest. So, we went back over to the previous room so that she could do an ultrasound. I was trying not to be agitated but I was hangry (hungry/angry). *Didn't I already go through this at Charlotte Radiology? I'm not paying y'all ass extra for the duplicate work.*

Once the ultrasound was done, the surgeon came in to perform the biopsy. She introduced herself and wanted to hear the story of how I found the bump. She looked at the ultrasound monitor to determine the best angle for surgery. As she did so, she seemed to be intrigued by my story and said, "I can't believe you found this." At the time, I didn't think much of it. Once she was done removing the tissue, she left the room for a few minutes. When she came back, she told me that the small mass was not a cyst. She went to say that she was unable to definitively provide a diagnosis without first sending the sample off to the pathologist. It usually takes 48 hours for the results. It was Thursday. I was told that I should hear something from them on Tuesday, no later than Wednesday. She placed a small metal clip to mark the spot so that it was easily identifiable for future procedures and sealed the area with surgical glue. Damn it! More waiting! Being in a state of limbo and the unknown led to many sleepless nights.

Despite what the surgeon told me, I felt it in my spirit that it was not good and that it was cancer. *I mean, what else could it be?* By Tuesday, I was a nervous wreck, so I was glad that I had an appointment scheduled with my hairstylist to keep my mind off things. Just as I was headed out the door the phone rang. "Mrs. Simmons, this is Atrium Health calling with the results from your biopsy. Your sample tested positive for Invasive Ductal Carcinoma; it is the most common form of breast cancer..." I zoned out. The nurse was still talking, but my mind was elsewhere replaying those words over again and again. Breast Cancer. I missed most of the conversation and by the time I zoned back into the call, I heard her say, "We need to get you scheduled for an appointment to see a breast cancer specialist."

Once the call ended, I immediately called Martin at work. "Babe, I need you! I need you to come home!" I could barely get the words out. I felt myself starting to hyperventilate, so I grabbed my inhaler. Once I was able to pull myself together, my very first instinct was sadness. Not because I had just gotten the worst phone call of my life, but sadness for my girls. Sadness because I may not get the opportunity to nurture them through adulthood, through marriage, pregnancy, or raising their kids. That was devastating. Because of the trials and tribulations with my mother, the relationship I have with my girls is everything to me.

My mother and I had a complicated relationship. When it was the most crucial time for a teenage girl to have her mother, she was not emotionally available. We were estranged for a few years and over time the mother/daughter relationship shifted. She began to view me less as a daughter and more as "just another woman on the street."

Those were her words, not mine. I believe she loved me in her own way, however, she got pregnant at 14, by a guy a few years older, who abandoned us before I was born. To this day, I've never met him, and I don't even know his name. Luckily, my mother had loving parents who supported her and stepped in to raise me while she continued her education. We lived with my Granny and Paw Paw until I was 12, then we moved into our place. Sadly, this is when the shift began.

When I met my husband, he encouraged me to mend my relationship with my mother. This was one of the reasons I fell in love with him. He was very instrumental in building the bridge between us. By the time she passed away in 2016, we had a great relationship. She was a phenomenal grandmother and absolutely loved my girls. I was happy that my daughters got to experience the love from her that I longed for as a teenager.

When Martin and the girls got home, I told them I got the call from the hospital letting me know that my biopsy results tested positive for breast cancer. Seeing the worry in my babies' face was unbearable. They tried hard to be strong for me, but we all were shocked and couldn't wait for my appointment with the breast specialist to find out treatment options. I later learned that they went into their rooms and cried. It saddened me to think that breast cancer would rob my daughters of precious time we had together.

When we arrived at the Levine Cancer Institute for my appointment with the breast specialist, Martin and I were optimistic. I felt perfectly normal and hadn't felt ill. I just knew they would tell me that a mistake had been made and that I had been incorrectly diagnosed. I low key considered getting a second opinion. I wasn't as anxious about that appointment as I was for previous appointments because I knew what to expect.

LCI assigned Margo as my nurse navigator. She had called me the week before to walk me through what to expect. We had also reached out to my cousin Marlo who is also a doctor and she made sure we were prepared as well. She ensured we knew the right questions to ask the doctor with regards to my case and was always available to answer any questions I had about Invasive Ductal Carcinoma or my treatment.

Dr. Voci, my breast specialist, came into the room with such positive energy; I loved it! The first thing she said was, "I have to hear the story about how you found the lump." After I finished sharing my story, Dr. Voci said, "That's incredible! I can't believe you found it; a mammogram never would have found this." She went on to say, "We got this! The mass is small enough to remove it surgically. You caught it early, you're at Stage 1!"

Martin and I were so relieved! If life had dealt the cards for me to have breast cancer, then Stage 1 was the best-case scenario. Dr. Voci went on to explain the next steps would be to have a lumpectomy. The surgery was to remove the tumor, as well as lymph nodes from my right breast. Afterward, it would be sent for testing to ensure that there were no cancer cells present anywhere else and test to see if there was a possibility for recurrence and what may have caused it. Everything sounded so simple, but the thought of being put under anesthesia terrified me. So many thoughts ran through my mind...*What if something goes wrong? What if I don't wake up? I watch Grey's Anatomy and I've seen those episodes! Before having kids, I used to be so fearless, and now I have so much to live for, I'm borderline paranoid.*

I shared with Dr. Voci that I did not know my biological father, so I do not know what health issues run in that family. Breast cancer does not run on my mother's side and I was concerned that my girls are at risk for this or any other cancer type. She told me about the genotype test which is done to identify traits that are passed down. She cautioned me that most insurance companies do not cover it, but that she would submit the order and present a good case as to why it was needed. Honestly, I didn't care if I had to pay out-of-pocket for it or the cost. Sign me up! A price tag can't be put on my girls' lives. Whatever the costs we would figure it out later.

I pride myself on being an authentic person and living my truth. I'm regularly active on social media, so I thought that it was important for me to post about what we were going through. Martin was against it, but I wouldn't be my authentic self if I only reported the good and not the bad. Plus, there are things that I've learned that I'm sure other women were not aware of that can potentially save lives. Specifically, regarding self-examination, dense breast tissue, and mammograms.

I was awestruck when Dr. Voci said that my lump never would have been detected by a mammogram since it was in the middle of my chest. When doctors teach you to do self-exams, they direct you to focus on the actual breast and around through the underarm. They do not mention that the upper mid-chest area is considered breast tissue and should be explored as well. Additionally, I did not know that I have dense breast tissue and certainly had no idea that it is a known fact that regular mammograms cannot see through dense breast tissue, which is common in women of color.

In my opinion, changes should be made, and regular mammograms should be scrapped altogether. Insurance companies should be required to cover the cost of diagnostic mammograms and/or ultrasounds for women with dense breast tissue. Early detection is key, and these two tests most accurately detect cancer.

When posting to social media, I was extremely transparent. It was very important to me that those reading my posts felt the same gut-punch effect that I had when I was diagnosed. So much so that they would be led to 1) Be intentional about their health, pay attention to their body, and go to the doctor. 2) Go get a mammogram. Inquire about dense breast tissue and request a diagnostic mammogram or ultrasound if needed. 3) Be inspired by my story to share it with others to educate others on a new way of doing self-examinations to expand the scope to include the chest area.

I was blown away by the overwhelming responses I received. So many people left words of encouragement, well wishes, and sent prayers up. I also received a ton of text messages and phone calls from people asking questions and wanting to know more. Although I didn't know my fate, I was excited and hopeful that by sharing my story, it would save someone else.

We are so incredibly blessed to have our village. There are so many of our friends and family rooting for me. Immediately after posting to social media, we began receiving an outpouring of love and support. My Jack & Jill Charlotte Sisters started a meal train. Loved ones sent flowers, cards, gift bags, breast cancer awareness T-shirts, alkaline water, scarfs, hats, and more. They did their research and sent all things to promote healing, mental health, and to keep our spirits lifted. A few people even sent financial support as well. We were so humbled by everyone's kindness and generosity and did not take it for granted. Many people do not have the support of family or friends and weather this storm alone.

On the eve of my surgery, I did not sleep at all. I had so much anxiety and was a ball of nerves. The ride to the hospital was somber. Martin and I didn't talk much; I was praying silently, and I suspect he was too. After checking in with the receptionist, I was so happy to see my sister-friend Natasha walk into the waiting room. It was God's way of saying "See, I got you!"

My sister-friend Natasha is Dr. Natasha Denny, OB/GYN on staff at the very hospital where I was having my lumpectomy. It put Martin and me at ease to see her. Natasha reassured us that I was in good hands and that I would be well taken care of. I knew that she would make sure I was. We were so grateful!

Within about two weeks, I was back in Dr. Voci's office for my follow-up appointment. I was still experiencing slight pain in my right breast and it appeared that there was fluid buildup. Other than that, the surgery had gone well. The tumor and lymph nodes removed were sent to the pathologist for testing and the results were back. The pathology report revealed that my nodes were negative, indicating that cancer had not spread.

However, there was a very small margin that showed cause for concern. Dr. Voci consulted with her fellows at the hospital and it was their recommendation for additional tissue to be removed. I'm not playing Russian Roulette with my life. So, another surgery was scheduled for the following week on July 16th, the day before my 49th birthday. Dr. Voci shared that pending the results of the Oncotype, she did not foresee me having to undergo chemo and felt strongly that radiation was all that would be needed for treatment. It was the best news ever! Dr. Voci drained the fluid from my breast and we were on our way home.

When I returned for the second surgery, I wasn't as anxious as before. Plus, I had established a great rapport with Dr. Voci, and I trusted her. Same surgery, but a different outcome. That time around, I didn't have an easy recovery. The pain started to kick in even before we made it home, which was only a 20-minute ride. Within a day or so, I was in excruciating pain and crying in agony. Martin called Natasha, who was such a doll, to stop by the house to check on me. There was redness and swelling in the area and it was hard to the touch, which indicated there may be an infection. It seemed to be fluid buildup in my breast again. It was after hours so Dr. Voci was out of the office, but we were able to reach Dr. Voci's partner who scheduled me the next day to have the fluid drained. Natasha had me ice the area which helped tremendously with the pain. I couldn't thank her enough for all she did.

A couple of weeks later, I had healed nicely and was consulting with my oncologist, Dr. Masterson. She thoroughly reviewed the treatment plan with us, radiation daily for 4-6 weeks and then Tamoxifen. She covered the side effects of Tamoxifen as well. Radiation was scheduled to start on August 9th. *Soon I will be cancer-free!*

The day I was scheduled to start radiation we were so pumped. That was my ticket to being cancer-free, or so I thought. When Martin and I got into the exam room the doctor came in. He was unable to proceed with the radiation treatment. My Oncotype was sent to my oncologist and the results indicated that I needed to report down to the main hospital. That only meant one thing chemo!

Dr. Masterson explained that my Oncotype came back at 43, which meant that I had an aggressive tumor with a high chance of recurrence. The best option for treatment would be chemotherapy first, then radiation. She went on to review the new treatment plan with us. Two rounds of chemo (Adriamycin and Cytoxan), every other week for eight weeks and then Taxol every week for 12 weeks to start on August 27th.

The most significant side effects of Adriamycin and Cytoxan are fatigue, hair loss, nausea, vomiting, and diarrhea. For Taxol, the side effects are hair loss, muscle and joint pain, neuropathy in the hand and feet, and low blood counts. She then scheduled me for my port placement and for a series of scans to be taken (CT, Bone Density and Echocardiogram).

The first round of chemo was difficult. I was so sick and incredibly fatigued that I was out of it and barely able to function. I had to have a blood transfusion because my blood count was extremely low. Then I started to notice subtle changes with my body and appearance.

Every day there seemed to be something new. I first noticed my nails turning black and my skin getting dark patches in certain areas. Then the hair loss. My armpits, arms and legs, vagina and then lastly my head. There was so much hair loss that it just didn't make any sense to hang on to it, so I decided it was time to shave what was left. Getting my head shaved was very emotional for me. My stylist BJ did the initial shave and my Hubby captured it on video. Everyone in the salon was being so encouraging but I cried the entire time. That was the defining moment for me when everything got real! *I have cancer and now I look like a person with cancer!* Going through that transformation was mentally challenging for me.

Everyone who knows me knows that I'm a fashionista and I love being impeccably dressed. My physical appearance is especially important and contributes to my self-esteem and confidence level. People who know me will find it hard to believe that I was an introvert as a child because I was teased for my appearance. As a toddler, I was disfigured from a freak accident that caused permanent blindness in one of my eyes. Classmates would call me the worst names and I often got into fights. I struggled with being accepted so, as an adult, this significant change in how I look took a toll on my mental psyche. But even during my darkest days, I knew I had to keep fighting. I had endured so much in my life and made it through. I survived molestation, rape, and domestic violence. Surely, I could survive Breast Cancer. I had too many people praying for me and pouring so much into me being better and winning that battle. There were even people praying for me whom I didn't even know. God is so Good!

My second round of chemo was one of the less aggressive chemo medicines, Taxol. The body aches and joint pain were more pronounced, but I pushed through. I was simply happy to be up and alert, and not be as out of it as I was on the previous medicine. The worst side effect for me was the neuropathy. There were times that I needed help getting dressed because I couldn't pull up my pants or needed help because I couldn't walk.

My last day of chemo was January 7, 2020. I made sure to dress cute for my turn at ringing the bell! Martin surprised me and arranged for my daughter, Courtney, to be there with balloons. He had also planned a special date night for just the two of us. We hadn't had one in months since my first surgery. I started radiation, the last part of my treatment plan. My genotype test came back negative for cancers, which means that my girls were not at risk.

My last day of radiation was on March 23, 2020. I am another step closer to being cancer-free. Unlike when I finished chemo, there was no fanfare, no ringing of the bell and my husband was not allowed in the hospital for safety reasons due to the global pandemic known as Coronavirus (Covid-19). So much has changed in the world and our new way of life consists of social distancing and sheltering-in-place. Although another victory is won, the battle continues. I am in the midst of a metamorphosis as my body rids itself of the chemo medicine and the burns heal from radiation, the side effects linger. The worst of the bunch are fatigue, muscle and joint pain, nerve damage, perimenopause, short-term memory loss, low libido, and lymphedema. Eventually, most of these will go away. Unfortunately, there is no cure for lymphedema, so it is here to stay. The swelling and pain will plague the right side of my body for the rest of my life. Treatment for lymphedema is daily. For no less than one hour, I am hooked up to a machine wearing a compression suit. This is my new normal. My next appointment with the breast specialist is in six months at which time a mammogram will be done. The expectation I have is that I will officially be declared cancer-free. In the meantime, I'm claiming it!

The doctor said that getting cancer is something like a fluke that just happened. But I believe that something bigger is in God's plan and I pray that He reveals my purpose for this journey soon. For now, I'll keep encouraging anyone who will listen to push for diagnostic mammograms and ultrasounds over regular mammograms because changes need to be made and early detection is key to saving lives!

As I sit here and reflect on the last few months, I'm reminded of the changes that have occurred since the discovery of my breast cancer. I put my business, Retro Chic Thrift, on hold to focus on healing. I'm grateful that my husband and I both work at companies with amazingly supportive managers and co-workers who are understanding and stepped in to pick up the slack. I'm reminded of how many times I felt like I was damaged goods, but today, I feel whole and beautiful and have embraced the hair loss caused by the chemo.

I'm reminded of the missed opportunities to enjoy precious time with people who were intentional about inviting me into their space to spend time with them. I'm reminded of the importance of friendship, the power of sisterhood, and to not take it for granted. We are so grateful for our friends, who are more like family. We were blessed to have women in my life who not only stepped into grocery shop and provided meals for my family but were also a source of strength when times were tough.

I'm reminded that I am loved unconditionally! My husband vowed to love me through sickness and health, and he has certainly done that! There are no words to adequately describe the strength, tenacity, and patience my husband showed while loving me through the worst part of my life. I'm reminded of my beautiful girls and how they love me so much that they put on brave faces to show no signs of weakness because they wanted to be strong for me.

Lastly, I'm reminded of the importance of staying connected to family and being deliberate in loving one another all the time and not just through tragedy. Martin and I are so thankful for the love and support from our families and can't thank them enough for all that they have done. We implore them to not sweat the small stuff, but instead love on one another as if it's the last day they will see each other.

For anyone challenged with battling breast cancer, or any life-threatening illnesses for that matter, my advice is to be transparent. Be open to share what you're going through: mentally, physically, and financially. Most important, ask for help without being embarrassed or feeling shameful, and accept support from anyone offering it to you! That includes family, friends, co-workers, church, hospital programs, etc. You will experience tough times, so having a support group is critical to your healing.

When you relieve your burdens to others and don't have to carry them alone, there is a shift in the atmosphere. I'm certain that had I not been transparent and posted my diagnosis to social media, my family and I would not have received the outpouring of love and support we received. This had a tremendous impact on my mental health, allowed me to focus on healing and helped me to stay positive.

Fight the fight, find the cure.

It All Started With a Promise

Susan G. Komen Los Angeles County
Circle of Promise Initiative
Arnedra L. Jordan
Public Health & Policy Consultant

    Addressing disparity issues in the African American Community can be difficult, complex, and challenging because no one wants to talk about the big secret or discuss what another family member may have died from. But in Los Angeles County, we believe that you must speak up and talk about breast cancer. We wanted to be an example of inclusion, diversity, citizen engagement, and advocacy. We wanted to teach African American women about the resources available to them in the community. This way African American women would have the tools that they needed to become proactive for their health and not reactive when they are diagnosed with breast cancer. The Circle of

Promise Initiative was created because of the myths and disparities that were happening in the African American community.

In 2010, Susan G. Komen Los Angeles County began the African American Taskforce. This group of citizens, breast cancer survivors and community advocates came together to discuss ways to change the story within the African American community when it comes to breast cancer. The main question that was addressed within this task force was why were African American women dying at such an alarming rate? Why were they diagnosed later and often with more aggressive breast cancer? Los Angeles county was committed to doing something that had never been done before. They went where African American women lived, worked, played, and prayed and took mammograms and other resources needed to live a healthy life directly to them. So, our work began to cut the disparities rates among African American women in Los Angeles County where African American Women are 56 percent more likely to die from breast cancer than their Caucasian counterparts, in sub-cities such as Long Beach that rate was 70 percent. This task force worked tirelessly to educate and empower the community. By 2012, the task force had provided over 1,500 no-cost mammograms to women and educated thousands of women through our Worship in Pink partnership with faith-based organizations.

In 2012, Anthem Blue Cross presented Los Angeles County with a challenge to continue to cut the disparity rates and to work even more within the community. This is how the Circle of Promise Initiative was born. Breast cancer continues to impact people from all backgrounds, but there are significant differences within the mortality rates among racial groups. During the early 1980s, breast cancer death rates for Caucasian and African American women were about equal, but during the 2001-2005 period, African American women had a 37 percent higher death rate. Susan G. Komen Circle of Promise has pledged to do our part to ensure that African American women are empowered with the information and tools they need to take charge of their health and serve as ambassadors in their local communities. The Circle of Promise movement is designed to engage African American women to help end breast cancer forever by fostering increased awareness, support, empowerment, and action.

Despite having lower breast cancer incidence rates across the nation, African American women's mortality rates are 41 percent higher than their counterparts. The same research indicates that African American women are often diagnosed at later stages, sometimes with more aggressive forms of cancer and at a younger age. The Circle of Promise initiative is working to change this reality. Using best practices informed by community leaders, conducting intensive peer-to-peer education where women live, work, shop, pray or play allows us to bring education and medical services to a community where none exist. Without it, thousands of women would not be screened, and thousands of women may have succumbed to the disease.

The Circle of Promise Initiative not only addresses breast cancer but covers the different sectors of the community in addressing challenges such as affordable housing to race equity issues to community-police relations. We are going beyond the traditional way of getting a mammogram and helping African American women get access. It all started with a promise. A promise that has evolved to something more than we could have ever expected. A promise that would help African American women to speak up and talk about and take a stand against systems that create limited access to good hospitals and doctors. Because people of color and low-income residents are disproportionately affected, creating healthy neighborhoods is our main priority.

Community Change

Our program provides a wide range of educational, basic health services for women and men in the community. The program brings licensed health care professionals, community partners, and breast cancer survivors together to help women participate in one of our many breast cancer health initiatives. Throughout the year, eligible women can receive free health screenings and treatment. Anyone in the community can participate in our education and public policy events.

Public Policy

We didn't just end there; we got together with community leaders, social justice organizations, and faith institutions. Komen Los Angeles County has worked to change laws that included barriers to African American women accessing treatment. Because of our Public Policy collective approach to addressing health disparities, we created real change within the community. Breast cancer treatment is expensive, and costs can add up quickly. In some instances, families might find themselves making the difficult decision to pay their rent or for their treatment. The Komen California Collaborative Public Policy Committee works to remove barriers such as these because no one should ever have to make that decision.

In 2013, California was the 27th state to pass the oral anti-cancer medication parity law, ensuring anti-cancer medications would be more affordable and accessible for cancer patients. Bill 1860 is a Komen sponsored bill that caps patients' out-of-pocket costs for oral anti-cancer drugs (oral chemotherapy). A.B. 1860 allows for breast cancer patients to choose if they want to take oral chemo or intravenous chemo and caps the pills at $250.00 per month. Komen Los Angeles County was proud to work, support and help this bill get passed in collaboration with the Komen National Public Policy Team and the Komen California Policy Collaborative. Before this bill, intravenous (IV) administered chemotherapy was covered by insurances at a more favorable rate than oral (pill form) chemotherapy, which made it difficult for breast cancer patients to access their oral chemotherapy prescriptions.

Our next task was to ensure that African American women in California who suffer from breast or cervical cancer and are uninsured or underinsured receive the treatment they need for their cancer by repealing the arbitrary treatment caps of the Breast and Cervical Cancer Treatment Program. The existing law requires the State Department of Health Care Services (DHCS) to perform various health functions, including providing breast and cervical cancer screening and treatment for low-income uninsured and underinsured individuals. Existing law prohibits "period of coverage" for the state cancer

163

treatment of people diagnosed with either breast or cervical cancer from exceeding 18 or 24 months. We were able to help convince the state to remove the cap and women can receive treatment for as long as they need it.

Komen Los Angeles is creating active partnerships with our community partners. These partners will help to get elected officials and local businesses educated around the public policies that may affect African American Women's breast health and develop incentives for African American women to make better health care choices.

Conclusion

As of 2020, Komen Los Angeles County has provided over 8,000 no-cost mammograms to women in the community in conjunction with our healthcare partners. We have educated millions of women and men in the county about breast cancer and early detection. We have created local partnerships with various health organizations, and we will continue to advocate for African American women until breast cancer is eradicated and there are no barriers in treatment.

What can you do to reduce your risk? DETECTION IS KEY TO SURVIVAL!

Ask your doctor which screening tests are right for you if you are at a higher risk. Have a mammogram every year starting at age 40 if you are at average risk. Have a clinical breast exam at least every 3 years starting at age 20, and every year starting at age 40.

*****

Help us rewrite the story of African Americans and breast cancer. Join the Circle of Promise now. We're encouraging you to Know Your Health to Know Your Self. For existing ambassadors, you will receive our Health Heritage Tree. This special family tree allows you to list your family members as well as any health conditions, i.e. cancer, diabetes, etc. We believe that understanding your family's health history will help you make healthy choices in everyday living. You can contact us at www. https://komenlacounty.org or you can reach me at ajordan@komenlacounty.org. Feel free to connect with me on Instagram: @proflawmaker.

About the Contributing Authors

Vonda Sumrall is a fourteen-year breast cancer survivor who works in the medical field. She's a devoted wife, mother of three, and she has one grandson.

Freedom LeMoi is a Chicago native and a free-spirited, optimistic mother of two, grandmother of three, and two-time breast cancer survivor. Free is a fear conqueror. Afraid of heights, she decided to go skydiving. The sky isn't the limit for this unstoppable woman!

Cheryl A. Brown is a native of Los Angeles. She has an effervescent personality coupled together with the passion and love of fashion along with the uplifting of women. This passion has allowed her to become a journalist, fashion blogger, motivator and now a published author. Cheryl is the mom of a beautiful daughter, Kristyn.

Tanya Ramsey is a Chicago Public School teacher. She has three master's degrees in Reading, English and Educational Leadership and is a graduate of Grambling State University. She has one daughter, Montana, who is sixteen.

Diane Drew Daniels is a Division Superintendent at Forest Preserve District of Cook County (FPDCC). She's a proud mother and grandmother. She's also an advocate for God!

Shanette Caywood is a single mother of two young men, ages 21 and 13. She is an advocate with the organization Living Beyond Breast Cancer and a Chicago Model of Courage. She served as an ambassador in South Africa with the organization A Fresh Chapter. Her diagnosis has taught her to live life with intent, passion, and purpose.

Antwone Muhammad is a youth guidance counselor, John Maxwell leadership coach, public speaker, recording artist, song writer, and two-time breast cancer survivor.

Lisa Boyd is a woman of God, entrepreneur, and CEO. After surviving breast cancer for the last three years, she created two businesses: Inspired By Faith NFP and Inspired By Faith clothing line. She's the mother of five and now an author!

Deshonjla Peterson is the wife to Kevin and mom to Kelsi and Zoë. She enjoys laughing hysterically, eating all the things that make you want to gossip about it, and working with people to ensure they know they don't have to navigate life alone. She also has an emerging coaching practice.

Kenya Johnson-Brown is the founder of LAG Spectacular Events. She holds an associate degree in business management. She is an amazing wife and mother of two kings, one queen and the proud grandma of three grandkids.

Andrea Simmons is a wife, mother, and entrepreneur. She's the owner of retro-chic Thrift Vintage Boutique. She and her husband of 27 years, Martin Simmons, currently reside in Charlotte, North Carolina with their three beautiful daughters Corinna (25), Courtney (20) and Morgan (16).

Glossary

Glossary terms used from American Cancer Society (www.cancer.org) & Cancer.Net (www.cancer.net)

Acellular dermis- a type of biomaterial derived from processing human or animal tissues to remove cells and retain portions of the extracellular matrix (ECM).

Acellular dermal matrix (ADM) - a soft connective tissue graft generated by a decellularization process that preserves the intact extracellular skin matrix.

Adriamycin, Doxorubicin, Red Devil - A chemo drug used to treat several different types of cancer. It works by slowing or stopping the growth of cancer cells.

Affordable Care Act and Cancer - The Affordable Care Act says most U.S. citizens and legal residents must have health insurance. Some states may charge fees to people who can afford health insurance but do not buy it. If you are unsure about the laws in your state, check the ACA website. Mammograms every year or 2 for women over 40. Companies must also pay for some other services to prevent breast cancer. For example, women with a higher risk of breast cancer can: See a genetic counselor to talk about breast cancer risk. Talk to a doctor about medication to prevent breast cancer. Regular screening for cervical cancer and the HPV vaccine to prevent cervical cancer. Help to stop smoking, such as counseling and medication.

Alloderm- tissue is sewn to the chest muscle to provide hammock-like support for the implant. The Alloderm tissue is essentially making the chest-muscle space larger, allowing a permanent full-sized breast implant to be inserted without having to use a tissue expander.

Anastrazole- a nonsteroidal aromatase inhibitor used in the treatment and prevention of breast cancer.

Anthracycline chemotherapy- medicines kill cancer cells by damaging their genes and interfering with their reproduction.

Aromatase Inhibitor- are a classic of drugs used in treatment of breast cancer in postmenopausal woman and gynecomastia in men.

Autologous or Flap Reconstruction- Uses tissue, skin, fat and sometimes muscle from another place on the body to form a breast shape. The tissue (called a "flap") usually comes from the belly, the back, buttocks, or inner thighs to create the reconstructed breast.

Advanced breast cancer- Means cancer is larger and has grown into nearby tissues or lymph nodes.

Benign- not cancerous

Bi-Lateral Mastectomy- total removal of both breast

Biopsy-Imaging studies such as mammogram and MRI, often along with physical exams of the breast, can lead doctors to suspect that a person has breast.

Biosimilar -a new type of biologic drug. A biologic drug or product is made from living things, such as antibodies or proteins.

BI-RADS (Breast Imaging Reporting and Database System)- reports the findings of mammograms, also includes information on breast density. BI-RADS classifies breast density into one of four groups: mostly fatty, scattered areas of density, consistently dense and extremely dense

Body lift perforator flap- reconstruction uses a flap of tissue from both sides of the lower abdomen (DIEP) and the upper buttocks (SGAP, or hip flap) to reconstruct the breasts — two flaps per breast, or four flaps in all.

Breast Prosthesis- breast forms intended to simulate breasts after a Mastectomy.

Breast self-exam- or regularly examining your breasts on your own, can be an important way to find a breast cancer early, when it's more likely to be treated successfully

BRCA Gene -Everyone has BRCA1 (Breast Cancer gene one) and **BRCA2 (Breast Cancer gene two) genes** - The function of the BRCA genes is to repair cell damage and keep breast cells growing normally. But when these genes contain abnormalities or mutations that are passed from generation to generation, the genes don't function normally and breast and ovarian cancer risk increase. Abnormal BRCA1 and BRCA2 genes may account for up to 10% of all breast cancers.

Breast Cancer- A cancer that forms in the cells of the breast.

Breast Reconstruction-a plastic surgeon creates a breast shape using an artificial implant (implant reconstruction), a flap of tissue from another place on your body (autologous reconstruction), or both.

By mouth- (orally) as a pill or capsule.

Cancer- is an uncontrolled growth of cells. Cancer occurs as a result of mutations, or abnormal changes, in the genes responsible for regulating the growth of cells and keeping them healthy

Carboplatin, Paraplatin - Chemo drug used to treat advanced-stage breast cancer and usually is given in combination with other chemotherapy medicines.

Catheter - (sometimes called a "long line") in your chest or arm. A catheter is a soft thin tube that is inserted into a large vein during a short, outpatient surgery. The other end of the catheter stays outside your body. This is basically the same as having a port, only you don't have the port itself. Your chemotherapy medicines are given through a special needle that fits into the catheter.

Chemo brain or fog -Many women who get chemotherapy to treat breast cancer say they have problems remembering, thinking, and concentrating during and after treatment.

Chemo Rounds- repeated cycles of when chemotherapy will be given ranging from 2-6 weeks

Chemotherapy-The use of drugs to destroy cancer cells. It usually works by keeping the cancer cells from growing, dividing, and making more cells.

Clinical trials -are used for all types and stages of breast cancer. Many focus on new treatments to learn if a new treatment is safe, effective, and possibly better than the existing treatments. The studies are done under careful supervision and they are FDA approved.

Compression sleeves and garments- are designed to do just what their name suggests: apply pressure to the arm, hand, or trunk to keep lymph moving in the right direction.

CAT, CT Scan, or computerized tomography scan- is an X-ray technique that gives doctors information about the body's internal organs in 2-dimensional slices, or cross-sections.

Cyclophosphamide, Cytoxan- A chemo drug used to treat several different types of cancer. It works by slowing or stopping the growth of cancer cells.

Cyst- a sac-like pocket formed in the tissue containing fluid, air, or semifluid matter. Most are benign.

DIEP Flap/Deep Inferior Epigastric Perforator Artery- Fat, skin and blood vessels are cut from the wall of the lower belly and moved up to the chest to rebuild the breast. It is very similar to a SIEA Flap, except that a different section of blood vessels in the belly are moved with the fat and skin.

Dense Breast -Have less fatty tissue and more non-fatty tissue compared to breasts that aren't dense.

Diagnostic Testing- (such as biopsy) are given to people who are suspected of having breast cancer, either because of symptoms they may be experiencing or a screening test result.

DCIS (ductal carcinoma in situ) - is the earliest type of breast cancer. DCIS is found only in the milk duct where the cancer started. DCIS is also called Stage 0 breast cancer and it isn't invasive.

Early detection- When abnormal issue or cancer is found early it is easier to treat. It has been proven to increase the chances of surviving breast cancer by about 30%.

Echocardiogram- is a graphic outline of the heart's movement.

Estrogen -female hormone.

Estrogen Receptor Positive - A cancer is called estrogen-receptor-positive (or ER+) if it has receptors for estrogen.

Excisions Biopsy - Removes the whole suspicious area, such as a mole or a lump.

Fam trastuzumab - an anti-HER2 medicine that has the same basic structure as Herceptin.

Fat Grafting, also called autologous fat transfer - is emerging as a new breast reconstruction technique. In fat grafting, fat tissue is removed from other parts of your body -- usually your thighs, belly, and buttocks -- by liposuction. The tissue is then processed into liquid and injected into the breast area to recreate the breast.

Fatigue - Fatigue is hard to describe. You feel like you don't have any energy and are tired all the time. But there's not a specific cause. It is the most common side effect of breast cancer treatment.

Free Tram Flap -fat, skin, blood vessels, and muscle are cut from the wall of the lower belly and moved up to your chest to rebuild your breast.

Fulphia -is indicated to decrease the incidence of. Infections manifested by febrile neutropenia.

Going Flat -Woman choose no reconstruction and don't wear a breast form most of the time.

Genotype - is a graphic outline of the heart's movement.

Grade - is a "score" that tells you how different the cancer cells' appearance and growth patterns are from those of normal, healthy breast cells. Your pathology report will rate the cancer on a scale from 1 to 3: Low, Intermediate and High.

Gynecomastia -swollen male breast tissue caused by hormone imbalance.

Heparin -A anticoagulant (blood thinner) that prevents the formation of blood clots, It is used to flush ports during chemo.

Herceptin, Trastuzumab - Is a targeted cancer drug for the treatment of cancers that have large amounts of protein called human epidermal growth factor receptor 2 (HER2). Herceptin works on the surface of the cancer cell by blocking the chemical signals that can stimulate this uncontrolled growth.

HER2 - cancer cells that do not have a large amount of a protein called HER2. On the surface.

HER2+- breast cancers make too much of the HER2 protein. The HER2 protein sits on the surface of cancer cells and receives signals that tell the cancer to grow and spread. About one out of every four breast cancers is HER2+. Herceptin works by attaching to the HER2 protein and blocking it from receiving growth signal.

Hormone Receptor Negative (no receptors are present), then hormonal therapy is unlikely to work.

Hot Flash - Sudden, temporary sensation of heat.

Hysterectomy - excision of the uterus.

Immunotherapy - Cancer immunotherapy medicines work by helping your immune system work harder or more efficiently to fight cancer cells. Your immune system is made up of a number of organs, tissues, and cells that work together to protect you from foreign invaders that can cause disease. Immunotherapy uses substances — either made naturally by your body or man-made in a lab — to boost the immune system to: stop or slow cancer cell growth, stop cancer cells from spreading to other parts of the body be better at killing cancer cells.

Inferior Gluteal Artery Perforator Blood Vessel /IGAP flap surgery - fat, skin, and blood vessels are cut from your lower buttocks and moved up to your chest to rebuild your breasts.

Implant Reconstruction -Inserting an implant filled with saline (saltwater) or silicone gel is placed either under the pectoral chest muscle or on top of the pectoral chest muscle. Using an implant to rebuild the breast requires less surgery than flap reconstruction. Incisional Biopsy-removes a piece of the suspicious are to study.

Inflammatory Breast Cancer (IBC) - is a rare and aggressive form of breast cancer. According to the American Cancer Society, about 1% of all breast cancer cases in the United States are inflammatory breast cancers. Inflammatory breast cancer usually starts with the reddening and swelling of the breast instead of a distinct lump. IBC tends to grow and spread quickly, with symptoms worsening within days or even hours.

Injection -a single shot into a muscle in your arm, leg, or hip, or under skin in the fatty part of your arm, leg, or tummy.

Intravenously (IV) - as a slow drip (also called an infusion) through a tiny plastic catheter in a vein in your hand or lower arm. A nurse inserts the catheter just before treatment starts and removes it when that treatment is completed. Tell your doctor or nurse right away if you feel any pain or burning while you're getting chemotherapy through an IV infusion.

Invasive Ductal Carcinoma or infiltrating ductal carcinoma - Invasive means that the cancer has "invaded" or spread to the surrounding breast tissues. Ductal means that the cancer began in the milk ducts, which are the "pipes" that carry milk from the milk-producing lobules to the nipple. Carcinoma refers to any cancer that begins in the skin or other tissues that cover internal organs — such as breast tissue. All together, "invasive ductal carcinoma" refers to cancer that has broken through the wall of the milk duct and begun to invade the tissues of the breast.

JP Drains – A closed-suction medical device commonly used as a post-operative drain for collecting bodily fluids from surgical sites.

Kadcyla -is a combination of Herceptin (chemical name: trastuzumab) and the chemotherapy medicine Emtansine. Emtansine, like some other chemotherapy medicines, disrupts the way cells grow.

Lapatinib, Tykerb - which works against HER2-positive breast cancers by blocking certain proteins that can cause uncontrolled cell growth.

Latissimus Dorsi Flap - an oval flap of skin, fat, muscle, and blood vessels from your upper back is used to reconstruct the breast. This flap is moved under your skin around to your chest to rebuild your breast.

Lobular carcinoma and lobular carcinoma in situ - Each breast has 15 to 20 sections called lobes, and each lobe has many smaller sections called lobules. Lobules end in dozens of tiny bulbs, which produce the milk carried by the ducts. Cancer that begins in the lobes or lobules is called lobular carcinoma and is more often found in both breasts than other types of breast cancer. Lobular carcinoma can be either in situ (remaining in the original location) or invasive (spreading to other parts of the body). When lobular carcinoma is "in situ," it rarely becomes invasive cancer, but having LCIS in one breast increases the risk of developing invasive cancer in either breast. In invasive lobular carcinoma, cancer has spread from the lobules to surrounding normal tissue and can also spread through the blood and lymph systems to other parts of the body.

Lumpectomy- Can preserve much of the appearance and sensation of your breast by removing affected breast tissue and it is a less invasive surgery.

Lymph nodes -are the filters along the lymphatic system. Their job is to filter out and trap bacteria, viruses, cancer cells, and other unwanted substances, and to make sure they are safely eliminated from the body.

Lymphedema - abnormal swelling that can develop in the arm, hand, breast, or torso as a side effect of breast cancer surgery and/or radiation therapy.

Lynparza - a capsule taken by mouth it is the first PARP inhibitor approved to treat breast cancer and is the first medicine approved to specifically treat breast cancers with a BRCA mutation.

Male Breast Cancer -very rare, with less than 1 percent of all breast cancers found in men. The risk increases for older men and those with high estrogen levels, low male-hormone levels or a family history of breast cancer. Increased risk is also associated with those who have been exposed to radiation, heavy drinkers, and those with liver disease or who are obese. Treatment options include surgery, radiation therapy, chemotherapy, hormone therapy and drugs that target genetic changes in cells that cause cancer.

Malignant - uncontrolled growth, Cancerous, invasive, metastatic.

Mammogram- mammogram creates a two-dimensional image of the breast from two X-ray images of each breast.

Mastectomy -The removal of the whole breast. There are five different types of mastectomy: "simple" or "total" mastectomy, modified radical mastectomy, radical mastectomy, partial mastectomy, and subcutaneous (nipple-sparing) mastectomy.

medullary carcinoma - usually a small tumor that is not aggressive and rarely spreads to the lymph nodes. True medullary carcinoma is quite rare and very difficult to diagnose with certainty, and some doctors may want to make sure they are not under-treating the cancer.

Metastatic breast cancer - (also called stage IV) is breast cancer that has spread to another part of the body, most commonly the liver, brain, bones, or lungs.

Menopause -the period of permanent cessation of mensuration.

Modified Radical Mastectomy -Involves the removal of both breast tissue and lymph nodes.

Monitoring tests- Once breast cancer is diagnosed, many tests are used during and after treatment to monitor how well therapies are working.

MRI, or magnetic resonance imaging- is a technology that uses magnets and radio waves to produce detailed cross-sectional images of the inside of the body. It is generally considered more sensitive for picking up breast cancer than mammograms.

Muscle-Sparing free TRAM flap - This means that your surgeon tries to use only part of the rectus abdominis muscle for the flap, instead of a large portion of the muscle.

Neulasta shot - injection prescription medicine used to prevent neutropenia.

Neuropathy - the general term for pain or discomfort caused by damage to the nerves of the peripheral nervous system.

Neutropenia - A lack of certain white blood cells caused by receiving chemotherapy.

Neutrophils - a type of white blood cell important in the body's fight against infection.

Nipple-sparing mastectomy - all the breast tissue is removed, but the nipple is left alone.

Oncologist - are doctors who diagnose and treat people who have cancer.

Oncotype DX test - is a genomic test that analyzes the activity of a group of genes that can affect how a cancer is likely to behave and respond to treatment

Oophorectomy – Surgical removal of one of both ovaries

Paget Disease - A rare form of breast cancer where disease of the nipple can cause pain and burning as an early symptom, along with irritation of the nipple.

Partial mastectomy - is the removal of the cancerous part of the breast tissue and some normal tissue around it

PAP Flap/Profunda Artery Perforator - uses this blood vessel, as well as a section of skin and fat from the back of your upper thigh, to reconstruct the breast.

Pathologist - a doctor who specializes in diagnosing disease based on examination of tissue

Pathologist report- tests on the tissue that is removed during a biopsy. These tissue tests not only tell you whether or not you have cancer, but also provide more information about the cancer itself and possible treatment options.

Pedicled TRAM -fat, skin, blood vessels, and muscle from your lower belly wall are moved under your skin up to your chest to rebuild your breast. The blood vessels (the artery and vein) of the flap are left attached to their original blood supply in your abdomen. Pedicled TRAM flaps almost always use a large portion of the rectus abdominis muscle.

Perjeta- is approved by the FDA to be used in combination with Herceptin and Taxotere (chemical name: docetaxel), a type of taxane chemotherapy, to treat HER2-positive, metastatic breast cancer that hasn't been treated with either Herceptin or chemotherapy yet

PET scans Positron Emission Tomography- can detect areas of cancer by obtaining images of the body's cells as they work.

Phantom Breast Pain - feeling pain in the breast that has been removed because the brain continues to send signals to nerves in the breast area that were cut during surgery, even though the breast is no longer there.

Phyllodes tumors -develop in the breast's connective tissue, which is called the stroma. The stroma includes the fatty tissue and ligaments that surround the ducts, lobules, and blood and lymph vessels in the breast. Phyllodes tumors of the breast are rare, accounting for less than 1% of all breast tumors. The name "phyllodes," which is taken from the Greek language and means "leaflike," refers to that fact that the tumor cells grow in a leaflike pattern. Other names for these tumors are phyllodes tumor and cystosarcoma phyllodes. Phyllodes tumors tend to grow quickly, but they rarely spread outside the breast. Although most phyllodes tumors are benign (not cancerous), some are malignant (cancerous) and some are borderline (in between noncancerous and cancerous).

Plastic Surgeon- A surgeon who specializes in reducing scarring or disfigurement that may occur as a result of accidents, birth defects, or treatment for diseases.

Port- (sometimes called by brand names such as Port-a-cath or Mediport) inserted in your chest during a short outpatient surgery. A port is a small disc made of plastic or metal about the size of a quarter that sits just under the skin. A soft thin tube called a catheter connects the port to a large vein. Your chemotherapy medicines are given through a special needle that fits right into the port.

Positive margin-cancer is present at the edge of the biopsy specimen.

Progesterone-is a hormone released by the corpus lute in the ovary.

Progesterone Receptor Positive- If it has progesterone receptors.

Prophylactic or Preventive Mastectomy- an elective operation to remove breasts so that the risk of breast cancer is reduced.

Quality of life-the standard of health, comfort, and happiness experienced by an individual or group.

Radiation Oncologist- a specialist physician who uses ionizing radiation in the treatment of cancer.

Radiation Therapy- The use of high energy x rays or other particles to destroy cancer cells.

Radical mastectomy - the most extensive type of mastectomy: The surgeon removes the entire breast, underarm lymph nodes and the chest wall muscles under the breast.

Receptor tests- tumor testing after biopsy or surgery for both estrogen and progesterone.

Reconstruction -the process of rebuilding after damage

Recurrence -return to a previous condition, repeated happening

Regimen- regulated course of, diet, exercise, or manner of living, intended to preserve or restore health or to attain some results.

Sciatica - Intense, sharp pain that radiates along the path of the sciatic nerve, which branches from your lower back through your hips and buttocks and down each leg.

Screening Test- (such as yearly mammograms) are given routinely to people who appear to be healthy and are not suspected of having breast cancer.

Sepsis – A life threatening complication or an infection. This occurs when chemicals are released in the bloodstream to fight an infection that triggers inflammation throughout the body.

SGAP Flap- Superior Gluteal Artery Perforator, or Gluteal Perforator hip flap, uses this blood vessel, as well as a section of skin and fat from your upper buttocks/hip (the so-called "love handles") to reconstruct the breast. Because no muscle is used, an SGAP flap is considered a muscle-sparing type of flap. The SGAP surgery removes tissue from high on the hip to avoid placing the surgical site in a potentially weight-bearing area, as the IGAP approach does. SGAP/hip flap surgery is more technically difficult than a TRAM, DIEP, or SIEA flap and usually takes more time to do.

Stacked DIEP flap reconstruction -is a newer approach to DIEP that can be used to reconstruct one breast in women who don't have a lot of extra belly tissue and therefore aren't eligible for standard DIEP surgery.

Side effects -any effect of a drug, chemical, or other medicine that is in addition to its intended effect, especially an effect that is harmful or unpleasant.

SIEA Flap/Superficial Inferior Epigastric Artery- Fat, skin and blood vessels are cut from the wall of the lower belly and moved up to the chest to rebuild the breast. It is very similar to a DIEP Flap, except that a different section of blood vessels in the belly are moved with the fat and skin.

Signal Transduction Inhibitor- drugs that may prevent the ability of cancer cells to multiply quickly and invade other tissues.

Simple or total mastectomy- concentrates on the breast tissue itself: The surgeon removes the entire breast. The surgeon does not perform axillary lymph node dissection (removal of lymph nodes in the underarm area). Sometimes, however, lymph nodes are occasionally removed because they happen to be located within the breast tissue taken during surgery.

Stacked/"Hybrid" GAP flap reconstruction - a newer approach to GAP that can be used to reconstruct one breast in women who don't have a lot of extra tissue in their buttocks and therefore aren't eligible for standard GAP flap surgery.

Staging - Helps describe where a cancer is located if or where it has spread. It also finds out the size of the tumor.

Surgery -Removes the tumor and nearby tissue during an operation.

Surgical Drain-implants that allow removal of fluid and organ from a wound or body cavity.

Surgical oncologist- A doctor who treats cancer with surgery.

Symptoms- a sign, evidence, or indication of something occurring.

Targeted Therapy- Targeted cancer therapies are treatments that target specific characteristics of cancer cells, such as a protein that allows the cancer cells to grow in a rapid or abnormal way. Targeted therapies are generally less likely than chemotherapy to harm normal, healthy cells.

Tamoxifen-SERMs block the effects of estrogen in the breast tissue by attaching to the estrogen receptors in breast cells.

Taxol, Paclitaxel- Taxol usually is given in combination with other chemotherapy medicines and is used after surgery to reduce the risk of early-stage breast cancer coming back. It treats advanced-stage breast cancer after it stops responding to standard chemotherapy regimens that include an anthracycline.

Taxotere/Docetaxel - It can treat breast, lung, prostate, stomach, and head and neck cancer.

TDM1, Kadcyla - used to treat HER2-positive metastatic breast cancer that has previously been treated with Herceptin and a taxane chemotherapy. Kadcyla also is used to treat early-stage HER2-positive breast cancer after surgery if residual disease was found after neoadjuvant (before surgery) treatment with Herceptin and taxane chemotherapy.

Testosterone -male sex hormone and antibiotic steroid

TRAM Flap /Transverse Rectus Abdominis - A muscle in the lower abdomen between the waist and the pubic bone. A flap of the skin, fat and all or part of the underlying rectus abdomens (6pack) muscle that are used to reconstruct the breast.

Triple-negative cancers can be more aggressive, harder to treat, and more likely to come back than cancers that are hormone-receptor-positive and/or HER2-positive.

TUG Flap/Transverse Upper Gracilis- Skin, fat, muscle, and blood vessels from your upper thigh is used to reconstruct the breast.

Tummy tuck- Plastic Surgery of the abdomen involving removal of excess fatty tissue and excess skin.

Tumors -abnormal growth in animate being.

Ultrasound -Ultrasound is an imaging test that sends high-frequency sound waves through your breast and converts them into images on a viewing screen

Vaccines -train the immune system to react to a specific target by exposing the immune system to the target or a weakened version of the target.

Xgeva, Denosumab - Xgeva is used to reduce bone complications and bone pain caused by advanced-stage breast cancer that has spread to the bone

Zarxio shots- stimulate the growth of neutrophils.

CPSIA information can be obtained
at www.ICGtesting.com
Printed in the USA
LVHW072030210920
666689LV00034B/1186